Federal architecture and fall foliage attract admiration on Fairfax Street.

A Guide to

Historic Alexandria

Second Edition

When it was founded, Alexandria, on its deep river channel, stood at the farthest point in British America to which one could conveniently journey inland from the sea.

William Seale

With Photographs by
Erik Kvalsvik

Over a century it grew into the busy river port shown in this Civil War view,
drawn in 1863, when the town was under Union occupation.

FROM THE COLLECTIONS OF THE MARINERS' MUSEUM, NEWPORT NEWS, VA.

Contents

Anne and Patrick Poirier's sculpture
"Promenade Classique" mirrors
the Washington skyline across the river.

Acknowledgments

To have such a book as this was the idea several years ago of Vola Lawson, then City Manager of Alexandria, and I hope it meets her expectations. I would like to thank Jean Taylor Federico, director, Office of Historic Alexandria; and in the Planning Department, Peter Smith, architectural historian.

Philip C. Brooks, chair, City of Alexandria 250th Anniversary Commission, and Patrick Henry Butler III, a member of the commission, were faithful readers and enthusiastic supporters of the idea of publishing a book for the anniversary. Ruth Lincoln Kaye's suggestions were also very helpful.

T. Michael Miller and William F. Smith, generous authors of the classic illustrated history *Alexandria Seaport Saga*, made countless contributions to this book. It is hoped that this book will whet historical imagination and lead visitors to the rich lore in that earlier volume.

At Time Life Books, Louise Forestall, Avakian Hrayr, Richard Hogg, Patricia Pascale, Carolyn Bounds, Virginia Reardon, and Kenneth J. Sabol saw the book through from inception to publication. At the Alexandria Library, Special Collections, Joyce McMullin, George Combs, and Kathy Chappell assisted in many ways. Lisa Odum at Mount Vernon, Sam Daniel at the Library of Congress, Howard W. Smith, Jr., Emily Coleman Kangas, and Sarah Graham Miller were helpful with particular aspects of the research. Special thanks to Cynthia Ware for a thoughtful review of the manuscript and advice.

Finally, many Alexandria homeowners and businesspeople provided information and access to their property in the course of my research for this book. They have my thanks.

William Seale

Introduction

Not **so long ago**, Alexandria was a small Virginia town very like other Virginia towns, deeply etched with traces of American history but no longer flourishing. Kinship and generations of friendship and acquaintance linked many of the houses and businesses, and gravestones in the cemeteries carried family names still heard in everyday conversation. Crumbling doorways, rambling alleys, closed shutters, and ancient trees lent a forgotten character to the place, while, as reminders of change, filling stations, five-and-dimes, and movie houses punctuated eighteenth- and nineteenth-century blocks of King Street and Washington Street. Cobblestones and brick, exposed in places, defied modern surfaces of concrete and asphalt.

Over a span of seventy years the old city has been transformed into a new one while keeping its quiet streets and rows of houses of brick and wood. Improvements, care, and restoration have created the Old Town Alexandria of today. Most visitors see only Old Town, but there is a great deal more to Alexandria. It is a city with suburbs, with a mayor and city council, schools, firehouses, humanitarian and everyday services. But the old and historic district is the symbol of the town that has survived the historic events of two and one-half centuries and, most recently, the pressures of dense population around Washington, which lies only a few minutes away. The town has often profited from its remarkable location; once it was the river, now it is proximity to the world's most powerful capital that makes it rich. Indeed, if one word summed up Alexandria historically, it would be "profit." Successful business established the city, maintained it, cleaned it up, repaired it, preserved and enlarged it.

New construction has been monitored in an effort to honor the old—which is essential to the city's character—and such an effort, laced as it is with abstractions, is sometimes a difficult fit in old buildings not designed for electric lights, air conditioning, and bathrooms. In this process there has been some delicate negotiation. The city's residents have cajoled and growled across the table. We have suffered some losses that are hard to tolerate even in memory. But we are proud of the result.

This book is a guide for visitors to Alexandria. It is for those who want to know more about the town. It describes events and personalities of the town's history as well as its most visible glory: its collection of architecture. Not all of Alexandria's architecture is great; but its predominantly nineteenth-century look makes it more cohesive than most towns, which are crazy quilts of buildings of all kinds. In many other historic towns, lesser structures have been weeded out, emphasizing the best architecture. Here the accumulation is of all classes. Alexandria is not a museum, although it has museums. For all its history, it is first of all a town where people live. It is a place of many layers for the visitor to explore. ■

Old Town Scenes

*Houses and gardens along
the historic streets present a variety of
approaches to living in row houses.*

*Pages 10–11: Market Square is
in full operation, as it has been for more
than 250 years.*

*Pages 12–13: A canopy of light adorns
King Street at Christmas.*

9

Alexandria, Virginia, 1853. In the distance, left,
the Potomac River, with the Maryland hills beyond it; right of
center, the approach to the town from Washington, D.C.,
Washington Street, the same thoroughfare used today.
Many structures that appear in this rare lithograph are still standing
and are familiar components of Old Town.

I Alexandria's Story

by W.H. & O.H. Morrison

ALEXANDRIA

1. River Village

*B*usinessmen founded **Alexandria.** Merchants saw in worn-out tobacco fields the end of a great colonial empire and sought a new beginning to replace an outmoded economic system. Struggling to survive, planters began to seed their fields instead with wheat and other grain crops, even as the merchants' vision reached beyond the furrowed earth to distant markets and other sources of wealth. Alexandria's story has always followed the same pattern of dramatic rise and fall. Today's painted trim and polished doorknobs evidence the glory of an upward swing.

The location on the Potomac River had already demonstrated its possibilities to the Dogue and Algonquin-speaking Indians, also commerce-loving people. The village that would become Alexandria was established not far from their trading villages, Nameranghequend—about where Reagan National Airport is today—and Assaomeck, Namassingakent, and Tauxenent, down the river southward. Captain John Smith took note of these Native Americans' business acumen,

Over the span of a century, Alexandria grew into the busy river port shown in this mid-nineteenth-century view.

In the eighteenth century, tobacco from outlying plantations was, by British law, graded and classified in Alexandria's warehouses before being shipped away to the ports of the world. The official warehouses proved to be gold mines for the town's merchants.

particularly at Tauxenent village, when he sailed up the Potomac in 1608, one year after the founding of Jamestown. Well within a century, English planters replaced the Indians, cultivated the land, and shipped their tobacco from the riverbank.

The site of present-day Alexandria was one of a number designated by the British crown after 1730 as shipping points for American tobacco. As part of an official effort to improve the quality of colonial tobacco, by law tobacco farmers had to submit their crops to inspection at these stations. For more than twenty years the existing village called "the town at

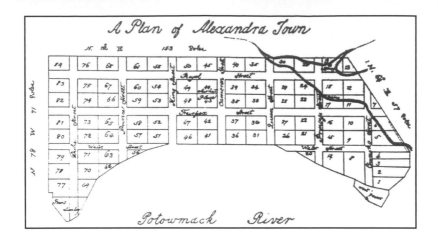

Alexandria was planned with streets and alleys on a strict grid pattern. The only public place, Market Square (opposite), had the first city hall, market stalls, and whipping post. From here, army and militia marched out King Street in 1755 to defend their king's claims to a backwoods empire.

Hunting Creek," for its location where that tributary flowed into the Potomac, was more a shipping and tobacco storage center than a town. It attracted representatives of British mercantile firms, who arranged the purchase of the tobacco and through whom credit was extended, the planters spending against the coming year's crop. In time the British merchants wished to increase their business with the Virginians and opened American stores selling British goods. A steady flow of people—many Scottish—came to the area to represent English mercantile houses. They found a ready market among Virginians.

*A*lexandria's role was to be a market town where people could go, stay over, and buy the merchandise on display in the stores. Georgetown, Maryland (now D.C.), whose earliest history was similar, would be laid out as a town two years after Alexandria. ∎

2. New Town

*W*ater transportation was the fastest and safest available at the time; nearly a century was to pass before railroads eclipsed it. The Potomac River offered a deepwater channel up to its rapids, 250 miles from Chesapeake Bay. It was the farthest a ship could navigate inland on a natural waterway in the Atlantic colonies. Alexandria thus stood at the most agreeable distant point from the sea, just below where rocky falls interrupted the navigability of the Potomac. In contrast to Georgetown, there were no rock outcroppings at Alexandria. The river presented a nearly perfect port.

Early Alexandrians looked both to the mother country and to the trans-Allegheny West. Local entrepreneurs saw opportunity in a water link between the ocean and the rich

THE ALEXANDRIA LIBRARY, SPECIAL COLLECTIONS (OPPOSITE AND ABOVE)

Market Square remains the town's public gathering place. The Saturday farmers' market brings enthusiastic crowds.

Such wooden houses as those in this slumping row were once a major feature of Alexandria. Most are gone today.

northwestern empire, the "Ohio country," by way of the Potomac. A journey north and west above Alexandria on the river took the merchants into close proximity with the rivers of the Ohio Valley, thus reaching more than 500 miles into the interior. Obstacles such as rapids and falls that blocked the way needed only canals and other improvements to bypass them, so the Potomac could become a golden highway for commerce between the new world and the old.

Fortunes were to be made as well in northwestern land speculation. Among the Potomac planters—most of whom were land speculators in one way or another—the appeal of the Ohio country amounted to a passion. A group of great planters formed the Ohio Company in 1747, sending agents to explore the frontier. Two years later the British government, encouraging private risk, granted 800,000 acres to the new company for development. In the year in between these two events, 1748, the entrepreneurs applied to the Virginia govern-

ment at Williamsburg for permission to build the town of Alexandria, named in honor of the Alexander family, who had held the patent on the land since 1669. The time had come to establish an important center of commerce.

*S*urveyors laid out the town of Alexandria in 1749. They platted the streets on a grid, as regular as graph paper, with the greatest thrift of space. One public place and only one was permitted—the Market Square—and it was for the conduct of business. Here a market house was built, a shingle-roofed shed, open sided at first, with stalls for shops. The city hall and an elevated, open plaza now occupy that same site, a few blocks up King Street from the river. Even the town pumps stood at intersections, so as not to waste land that might bring in money. (History usually attributes this economy to the Scottish character—there being many Scots in the neighborhood—but tightfistedness was not limited to

George Washington's town house on Cameron Street
is seen here as reconstructed in the 1960s.

them.) Otherwise, every inch of the town plan was lots for sale, to be used for residences, stores, warehouses, or taverns.

The grid lines were not always straight; occasionally, to this day, across-the-fence neighbors are seen at lawyers' tables or in court disputing a few square feet of property. The street names reflected the times: Royal, King, Queen, Prince, Princess, Duke (just the single words, giving no specific identification of actual personages); Pitt Street, for William Pitt, Earl of Chatham, the great political friend of America; Fairfax, for the mighty Fairfaxes of Belvoir plantation (now Fort Belvoir), lords of Virginia's Northern Neck and kin of British peers. They were the richest landholders in the colony. Cameron Street was named either for the

legendary Scottish chieftain or again for the Fairfaxes, who were the barons of Cameron; St. Asaph, for the bishop of St. Asaph, pamphleteer in support of American causes; Oronoco, for a species of tobacco grown by the local planters. Water Street, of obvious inspiration, rambled along the docks at the river.

The Potomac River's ragged bank formed a ridge varying from as low as three feet to as high as twenty feet, with mudflats between the elevated shore and the river itself, so some lots were high and dry and others so low as to be in marsh or even under water. To hold title to a lot, the owner had to erect within a set period of time a building of brick, stone, or wood, at least twenty by twenty feet. Houses were built, though not a large

number; later fire insurance maps of the town, showing the locations, materials, and footprints of the buildings, suggest that a number of early houses, with square plans reflecting the minimum dimensions and nearly all of wood, survived into the twentieth century. The heaviest investors built houses as anchors to the new town. Merchants built first, notably facing Market Square on the west, and to the east, beyond the steep riverbank, looking across the Potomac to the Maryland hills on the other side. William Ramsay's Dutch-gable cottage of milled lumber today stands reconstructed at the corner of King and North Fairfax Streets. Next door, the merchant John Carlyle, a Scot reared in the north of England, built a lofty stone house that would have been at home in the Lowlands of Scotland. His wife, Sally, was a Fairfax, and Carlyle, elevated by marriage, felt justified in a little domestic show, which he enjoyed in the splendor of elegant wood-paneled rooms. ∎

John Carlyle, the preeminent merchant of colonial Alexandria, built his house of rubble and dressed Aquia sandstone, quarried downriver. His portrait hangs over the fireplace in his fine Georgian parlor. Here the colonial governors met with General Edward Braddock on April 14, 1755, to plan a military campaign against French aggression on the western frontier.

3. Alexandria & the Northwest

*I*nternational politics now intervened. The French, who claimed the Ohio country as their own, had sent an expedition to the Ohio Valley in 1749 to secure the crown's position. Agents of the Ohio Company hurriedly established protected warehouses at present-day Cumberland, Maryland; then at Redstone Creek, Pennsylvania; and last, well into the interior at Fort Prince George, at the forks of the Ohio River, where Pittsburgh stands today. A second company from Virginia, the Loyal Company, with a grant from Williamsburg, also moved employees into the valley. The stage was now set for conflict.

Difficulties with the French in the Ohio Valley increased as the imperial struggle between England and France grew. The post yet unfinished on the Ohio fell into French hands. Twenty-one-year-old George Washington, a well-known local youth but not the rich planter of later years, was dispatched by the royal governor

to take an ultimatum to the French that they honor the company's claims and withdraw to Canada. John Carlyle recorded the result: "When he delivered his letters & etc. to the French Commander his Answer Was he was their by order of the Commander of the French at Qebeck & should stay." This Washington reported in January 1754 to the governor at the palace in Williamsburg. Governor Dinwiddie admired the pluck of the "raw laddie." When he and his council decided to send troops to make a stronger point with the French, Washington was put in charge.

Young Washington soon felt the results of fame. His name became known throughout the colonies. Although his hometown is universally considered to be Alexandria, he lived at Mount Vernon, two hours away by river. This large farm had come to him

The Washingtons of Mount Vernon, depicted here in their younger years, Martha (by John Wolleston) at the time of her first marriage and George (by Charles Willson Peale), at forty, in his Virginia militia uniform. The trunk (opposite) is fitted for travel tableware, and the couple presumably dined with its dishes and cutlery during the freezing winter at Valley Forge.

recently in a line of inheritance from his father through his late brother. Ambitious to make money and mindful of rising to the high level of distinction of his proud friends among the gentry, he provided youthful energy and enthusiasm for the Ohio Company. What would be called "Potomac fever"—the passion to make the river into a passage to the West—possessed him as it had the many others with whom he shared the vision. This he never surrendered, and, through him, the idea influenced the course of America's history, as well as Alexandria's.

Washington was tall and powerfully built but was a graceful man in the saddle or on the dance floor. That he was born to lead was clear, long before his years of fame, to most who were qualified to judge. For the Ohio expedition he drilled his men in Alexandria. The merchants came forward as outfitters for the militiamen, not oblivious of the double joy of profit and the security of their investments in the Ohio country. In addition, Virginia's counties had contributed 10,000 English pounds.

*O*n April 2, 1754, the militia assembled on Market Square and marched out King Street, northwest from Alexandria, with Washington at the head. Three months later they faced a superior force of Frenchmen and Indians at Fort Necessity, near Fort Prince George, and surrendered after a devastating battle. France, meanwhile, seeing the threat to her American possessions, sent 3,000 troops. The British responded by sending Major General Edward Braddock as commander of British forces in America. He arrived at Hampton Roads on February 20, 1755, with 1,500 British regulars and in freezing weather went on to Williamsburg, where Governor Dinwiddie presented him with a ton of worries. Among these were the lines of military supply, which were largely in the hands of the Alexandria merchants. For all the big bills they sent and the profit they were making, the merchants were not delivering provisions at a satisfactory rate.

*F*rom Williamsburg, Braddock ordered his regulars, militia, and supplies to Alexandria for a busy winter. Stockholders in the Ohio Company sought his sympathy. General Braddock and Governor Dinwiddie requested that the governors of other colonies obtain funds from their legislatures and called a meeting of colonial governors for April in Alexandria.

By winter's close, soldiers, along with throngs of onlookers and militia families coming to visit, packed the rugged new town to its eaves. For the first time Alexandria seemed like a populous place. The local people found the British obnoxious. "By Sum means or another," wrote John Carlyle, "[they] came in so prejudiced against Us, our Country, &c. that they used us Like an enemy's Country & Took every thing they wanted & paid Nothing or Very little for it, & When Complaints was made to the Comdg Officers, they Curst the Country, & Inhabitants, Calling Us the Spawn of Convicts the Sweepgs of the Goals & c. which made their Company very disagreeable." British officers orchestrated a show of military might, with drilling on Market Square and marching through the Alexandria streets.

The governors of four colonies—Massachusetts, New York, Pennsylvania, and Maryland—and Governor Dinwiddie himself assembled in April. For the meeting place, Braddock rented John Carlyle's new house overlooking the river for fifty pounds. Carlyle wrote: "Their was the Grandest Congress held at my House ever known on This Continent. . . ." The host did not like the guest, savior of Ohio though he might be: "A Man of Week understanding, Possitive, & Very Indolent, Slave to his Passions, Women & Wine, As Great an Epicure as could be in his Eateing, Tho' a brave Man." The governors wrote proposals to the crown for a new system of colonial taxation to cover frontier defense and bid Godspeed to General Braddock. In the radiant spring the troops left Alexandria and marched toward and across the mountains, headed for disaster. They met a surprise attack about ten miles from the forks of the Ohio River. Braddock died in battle (some say, killed by one of his own men) and was buried in the road, to hide his remains from the Indians.

His aide-de-camp, George Washington, fought with cool determination, gaining universal admiration. Washington had fired the first shots of what Europe knew as the Seven Years' War, in America the French and Indian War. He returned home and was given command of all the troops in Virginia. But while still in the Ohio country he had decided to make major changes in his life. He resigned his military duties in 1758 to take his seat in the Virginia House of Burgesses. In the same year he married the widow Martha Dandridge Custis, taking her and her two children to Mount Vernon to live, and, through her, coming into control of one of the largest estates in Virginia. ■

4. British No More

*T*he close of the war in 1763 transformed the British colonial empire. For America, the year was a watershed, and for Alexandria, it meant that the Ohio country was open. A vast Northwest stretched virtually untouched before the entrepreneurs. Alexandria's location on the edge of the frontier brought ever greater opportunities. Through the 1760s and 1770s, businessmen moved to town in large numbers. Many were merchants only; others were planters who, like Washington, were not opposed to dabbling in trade. But their office walls were plastered with maps. Land in the northwest was the all-consuming subject of conversation.

The town grew. Institutions that had served it from afar were established locally, notably the Church of England. Worship was not restricted to the Anglican church, for the Scots were Presbyterians. But it was the church sanctioned by the government and supported by public money. Already in the early 1750s an Anglican "chapel of ease"—a convenient chapel—had been established in

Alexandria. Today's Christ Church was built just outside the city limits in 1773, a beautiful Georgian image in architecture executed in brick trimmed in stone from the Aquia Creek quarry, downriver from the town. Christ Church (which was not named that until 1812) was supported by tithes, or church taxes. In addition to its spiritual duties, it was charged with the care of the poor and other humanitarian needs of the area it served. "Glebe" land was granted to support it. Sitting in the great, solitary room of Christ Church today with its thick, white-plastered walls, the lines of windows neatly incised, one can easily imagine being in a parish church in England. At no other spot in eighteenth-century Alexandria is the British Empire so vividly recalled.

Christ Church, which gained its name only in the early nineteenth century, was the Church of England when the congregation was founded in the 1750s and this church building was completed in 1773. Altered in the 1860s, it was restored as shown at right in the 1890s. The silver plate, installed during the restoration, marks the pew of George Washington. The obelisk is in memory of early Alexandria contractor Charles Bennett.

*T*he British economic system bound its colonies to support the mother country by serving as satellites supplying raw materials to manufacturers at home. Concurrently, the colonies provided a market for British manufactures. After the war's close in 1763, the British took a new look at this so-called mercantile system and modified it to reap more revenue. The result was loathed impositions upon the colonists, including the Stamp Act, which kindled first protest, then anger and defiance. The Declaration of Independence was proclaimed a mere thirteen years after the war that won the Ohio country. Alexandria's George Washington, of whom the broader world had heard before, was to lead the Americans to victory.

Alexandria never became a battleground in the American War for

Independence. The citizens ran scared from the beginning to the end, certain that the British could conceive of no finer plum than the river city. Two weeks after the Declaration of Independence was signed, Alexandrians were horrified by news that the British warship *Roebuck* was at Fredericksburg and on its way upriver. Captain Robert Conway and a party of men rowed out to watch for the ship. They lost their nerve when they saw it and, unarmed, scrambled ashore in Maryland to hide. The ship went ashore a distance below the town, where the troops aboard burned and looted all that was at hand, then departed.

*T*hough safe for the moment, Alexandrians were alarmed by what they considered a close call. With stores brimming with merchandise and a lively market promised by war, they wanted protection. First they built a garrison and hired troops to man it. Two companies of Minute Men defended river and town. Later, various militia companies replaced them. Eventually the city fathers drafted men who had stayed home, stirring loud objections. Toward the very end of the war, a small fleet of British ships flying French flags as a disguise did appear before Alexandria's docks. People began fleeing the town, taking their possessions, crowding the roads. The head officer of the county flew the colors, expecting the draftees to come to his aid, which they did not. Persuaded to lower the flag, he, with others who remained, lay low, and the ships went away. All Alexandria actually suffered was harassment.

The War for Independence proved to be profitable for the businessmen. Armies passed through Alexandria, and the merchants squeezed every penny they could from the soldiers and the government with almost religious fervor. They maneuvered Alexandria into position as a center for smallpox inoculation (at that time a new but proven treatment) for both soldiers and civilians; in one five-day period 975 troops were inoculated. The merchants sold supplies and, despite the war, carried on a profitable trade with the larger world. Commerce with the West Indies was lively. The merchants filled their shelves with rum and English and French goods.

They also outfitted Alexandria's audacious privateer *George Washington*, which sailed out of the port of Alexandria in the spring of 1778, to dock in France a mere eighteen days later. While departing Chesapeake Bay, the ship attacked and captured a British privateer, which, in the charge of several crew members, was sent on to Philadelphia to be sold for profit. After a winter harbor near Nantes, the *George Washington* set out in the Atlantic in the spring and made its way along the coast of Spain. Entering Chesapeake Bay at Cape Henry, it easily captured a large British privateer. The *George Washington*'s glories were many. One of its sailors, William Dove, remembered bitterly that the merchants never gave the crew the customary prize money.

Victory came at last, and peace and joy blanketed the town. In July 1782, marching north from the October victory at Yorktown, French troops under General Rochambeau

*Eighteenth- and early nineteenth-century warehouses
along Union Street, now restaurants and shops, sometimes give
evidence such as this, of earlier purposes.*

passed through Alexandria and camped on the meadow just outside town where General Braddock's men had pitched their tents. It was scorching hot. To cool down, the Frenchmen stripped to their long-tailed shirts, and the "most elegant and handsome young ladies" of Alexandria, without "the least embarrassment," came out and danced with them on the grass.

With the long war over, Alexandrians began to grasp the immensity of their achievement—and did not overlook America's debt to the hometown boy. On Christmas Eve 1783, Washington returned to Mount Vernon. On New Year's Eve he agreed to come into town, and an ecstatic Alexandria greeted him with thirteen blasts from the town cannon. The mayor spoke of "the inestimable Services which you have rendered your Country," and continued: "Attached to your Person by a long Acquaintance with your Virtues, it is and shall be our Prayer, that Heaven may preserve you in Health, and prolong a Life, which it has decreed that should be of so much Importance to Mankind." The general's response was every bit as tropical; but after his farewell address in Annapolis, his audiences had high expectations. In enduring Alexandria fashion, the event concluded with a big subscription dinner at Duvall's Tavern and plenty of toasts, not the least a cup raised to "uninterrupted trade with the world." ∎

Silver days: Adam Lynn, above, made the likes of such cake baskets as this for Alexandria's gentry. Benjamin Barton, a rival, occupied this shop on King Street.

5. What the Town Was Like

*A*fter the Revolution, **Alexandria came into its own as a town.** Even during the war the city fathers were alert to the need for changes. As wartime wealth came to the merchants, they sponsored new laws that cut off the political control that the country gentry had held over city offices in Alexandria for years and placed it in townspeople's hands. To serve as an elected official of Alexandria, one now had to live in the town. The townsmen now mastered their own fortunes.

George Washington, although one of those ousted, maintained a warm interest in the town. He endowed the new Alexandria Academy so that it could also offer free education to poor boys and girls. He took a great interest in the Friendship Fire Company, and it is said that on one of his visits to town, on seeing the volunteer firemen rushing to a blazing McKnight's Tavern on King Street, he dismounted from his horse, leapt up on the engine, and helped put out the fire.

Alexandria's enviable prosperity under independence continued off and on for forty years. A glance at a map of the United States in the 1780s and 1790s reveals how central Alexandria was. It was situated just about in the middle of what was then the United States, and this prime location, then as now—although for wholly different reasons—became its economic trump card. Entrepreneurs were attracted

Advertisement in the Alexandria
Gazette, *1800*

both by the wealth it had attained and
by the promise of its geographic
position.

You can still visit the town of
those days, developed between 1780
and 1820. Of course, new houses and
businesses have been built since then,
but Alexandria still leaves a strong
physical impression of its earliest
heyday. Take a walk down Prince,
King, Fairfax, and Duke Streets,
among the lines of tall, rectangular
houses the merchants built in the thirty
or forty years after the American
Revolution. They are an interpretation
of English Georgian architecture, not
unlike their contemporaries in
Philadelphia and Baltimore, but
smaller and typically more restrained
in their ornament. If John Carlyle's
house would blend easily into the
outlying neighborhoods of Edinburgh
in Scotland, then the merchants'
houses of Old Town might cause a
brief pause in Canterbury, being close
in appearance to the indigenous
houses of that cathedral town, but
slightly different.

Alexandria's early residences
and shops look somewhat alike and
share a tradition of fine materials and
construction. The early town was
plentifully supplied with men in the
building trades. Especially in the

1790s, attracted by the major building
projects of the new capital across the
river, builders flocked here from
England, Ireland, Italy, Scotland, and
all over the United States, and a
flourishing Alexandria offered a ready
source of clients that continued for
thirty years. Carpenters, bricklayers
and stonemasons, glaziers, ironwork-
ers, painters, roofers, joiners—all were
here, both white men and black,
freedmen and slaves, and their skill
can be seen today in Alexandria's
early architecture. Building products
came from England as well as the
United States—iron and brass locks,
nails, screws, hinges, window glass,
even ovens and stoves. Bricks were
usually made locally. Wood might
come by boat from the forests and
mills of the Northern Neck of Virginia
or North Carolina.

*A*lexandria's late eighteenth-
century houses rose one,
two, or three stories over a cellar, with
an extra floor tucked away beneath the
eaves and lighted by dormer windows.
They were not pretentious houses.
John Carlyle's freestanding house,
several row houses, and a few mansions from subsequent periods were
exceptions to a practice of restraint. In
a typical early Alexandria house, not
an inch of space was wasted, nor were
more inches built than necessary.
Alexandria cellars cause you invari-
ably to bump your head; Alexandria
attics force even short people to duck.
Meager hallways, steep stairs, and an
economy of windows extend the
penury. But the fireplaces are generous, allowing for big logs. Even
modest houses boasted louvered
shutters to control the light and air.

Early Alexandrians kept warm in winter and cool in summer in the days before mechanical climate control reduced the effort to adjusting a thermostat.

The early houses typically open directly from the street into a very narrow corridor that widens into a stair hall—never ample—at the back of the house. A shop or office on the ground floor likely required a second front door or a broad show window, and some of these still exist. Where there was a shop in front, most of the residential quarters were upstairs, with kitchen facilities in a narrow rear wing. Neither bathrooms nor closets complicated plans of the early times. A back stair served family privacy, providing a connection between the kitchen and the living area. The principal room—the largest in the house—was usually on the second floor in front, running the full width of the house and serving as a parlor. Bedrooms, or "chambers," were the other upstairs rooms.

*I*n the yard in back, within high wood fences or brick walls, many household activities took place where patio gardens bloom today. Clothes were washed there, boiled in pots and hung out on lines to dry. Chickens and ducks were kept in cages, and dogs and cats wandered in and out the open doors. In the corner stood the inevitable privy. Some of the more ambitious of these were of brick with louvered windows and plastered interiors, encasing plentiful seating. The larger houses might have stables, with space for groom, horses, and a carriage or two; a few small stables survive. An example of a fairly

average eighteenth-century stable can be found at the end of the garden of Benjamin and Elizabeth Dulaney's house at 601 Duke Street, opening on to Duke Street. But livery stables were more numerous in Alexandria than private ones. Most townfolk walked in any case.

Shops and offices were a pre-dominant feature of this commercial center. They are best remembered in the Stabler-Leadbeater Apothecary Shop, one of the nation's finest, which was established in 1796 and continued in

Gadsby's Tavern, one of the great hostelries of the early nation, was managed by a succession of tavernkeepers, including John Gadsby (above). The courtyard (opposite, below) is shown on hard times in the late nineteenth century, while the silver spoons and forks give a glimpse of Gadsby's hospitality in its heyday. At the corner of North Royal and Cameron Streets, the old tavern today is a museum and restaurant.

GADSBY'S TAVERN MUSEUM (OPPOSITE); THE ALEXANDRIA LIBRARY, SPECIAL COLLECTIONS (ABOVE)

business for 141 years. It remains virtually intact with its original contents. Although its drugstore paraphernalia have survived from both the eighteenth and the nineteenth centuries, the structure itself dates from the early nineteenth century. Perhaps a hundred shops in early Alexandria were more or less like the apothecary, selling a wide variety of other types of merchandise and equally full of wares but dissimilar to any store we might enter today.

We know from newspapers and old inventories that Alexandria's merchants had plenty on hand to sell—India or British cotton or Canton or French silk for a dress, calico for curtains, feathers for hats, and golden galloon to make a militia officer's uniform something to dazzle the eye. Some mercantile houses had supplies of hardware; and the Alexandria archaeologists have found huge and varied quantities of glass and porcelain everywhere. At 112 South Royal Street is the house of Joseph and Henry Ingle, cabinetmakers, who made furniture for Thomas Jefferson. Until recently, the locations of original counters and shelving could be traced on the broad-plank pine floors. The Ingles' furniture, made in this home shop, can be traced in the account books of early Alexandrians.

Another feature of the early townscape was the taverns. There were a lot of them, and they flourished and declined according to the merits of table and bar. They differed little in appearance from houses, except that the finer ones were much larger than Alexandria houses. Within, they were hives of activity, their furnishings moved around constantly to accom-modate a wide variety of uses. Guests were treated more or less as visitors to a private home, although crowds often put total strangers in family-style circumstances. They shared beds and sat down at common tables to devour platters of pork chops submerged in sweet syrup, ham, a profusion of seafoods—notably oysters and fish—corn, greens, and fruit from the Market Square, breads, and all the other delights of the day. Old inventories list barrels and cases of wine. The well-stocked bars of the taverns also provided generous supplies of beer, ale, whiskey, and gin, and a large assortment of each.

*C*rowds of convivial patrons found fine entertainment at the taverns of John Gadsby and John Wise, the main ones forming the complex called Gadsby's Tavern, still standing at Royal and Cameron Streets. This tavern was familiar to the first five presidents of the United States. Jefferson and his vice president, Aaron Burr, celebrated their victory in the seminal election of 1800 at Gadsby's with Alexandria citizens, who had voted for Jefferson but, soon to become residents of the District of Columbia, would not be able to vote in another presidential election for nearly fifty years. The glory of Gadsby's is defined in the inventories its owners left, listing what it took to run a first-class hotel in this busy river port of the early nineteenth century: scores of glass tumblers, stacks of trays, tablecloths and napkins, chamber pots, large numbers of beds, and mountains of bedding.

The heart of the city in the prosperous years following the

Revolution was Market Square, where crowds gathered, politicians orated, militia mustered, farmers brought their garden products for sale, and felons were whipped, cropped, and branded. City fathers built there a fine city hall, with market stalls in arcades at ground level and a very handsome clock tower. The much larger City Hall of today was built on the ashes of the original, which burned on May 19, 1871; citizens insisted that the old clock tower be copied to the inch, and an enthusiastic citizen, John Bathurst Daingerfield, paid for it. You can see where the earlier market house arcades are suggested in the brick arching around the base of the building. Today's Market Square, while it still has markets, serves the town in a ceremonial function, as well as remaining a gathering place for festivals, rallies, speeches, art shows, antiques fairs, and an occasional rock concert.

Downhill from Market Square is the port, which still receives seagoing vessels, although not to the extent that it once did. Lines of sailing ships and, later, steamboats characterized old days in the port, which was faced by commercial buildings, many of which survive as shops and restaurants.

Ropewalks and sail lofts, supply houses, warehouses, and the components of a busy port clustered around the Alexandria waterfront. Seamen's "ordinaries" kept the constable busy, when the port was full. Fights and murders called up stern warnings from the town fathers. A traveler who visited Alexandria in 1784 remembered seeing two severed heads displayed on pikes above the chimneys of the jail. ■

6. Alexandria, D.C.

*N*ational events brushed against the town. At Alexandria began the path that led to the creation of the United States Constitution. A six-man commission from Virginia and Maryland met in City Hall's Assembly Room on March 28, 1785, seeking to agree on rules governing the use of the Potomac River and Chesapeake Bay, which they shared and over which the central government had no regulatory power. This meeting's agenda demonstrated that the government of the Confederation, which bound the United States together after the Revolution, was too focused on the independence of the states individually to address effectively matters of concern to all. States had to settle among themselves problems that, under a stronger central government, might have been decided with facility.

George Washington, one of many farsighted men who were deeply troubled over the inadequacy of the Confederation, invited the commissioners at the Alexandria meeting to adjourn to Mount Vernon. Under his hospitable roof, the maritime problems were quickly settled, and General Washington turned conversation to broader topics. The commissioners decided to continue discussions at a second meeting at Annapolis, Maryland, and to invite representatives from all the colonies. After Annapolis, a third meeting, held in Philadelphia in May 1787, evolved into the Constitutional Convention, which created the

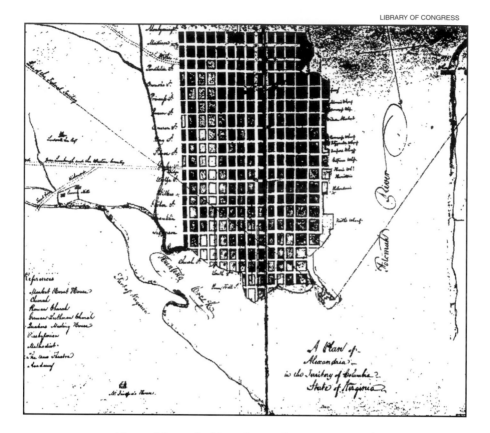

*Alexandria, tucked into the southernmost part of
the District of Columbia in 1801, reaped few advantages from the
federal district. In 1847, forty-six years after entering D.C.,
local citizens rejoiced over being returned to Virginia.*

compact by which Americans live today.

Alexandria's planter gentry distinguished themselves: George Mason's Virginia Declaration of Rights became the precedent for the Bill of Rights, the first ten amendments to the Constitution. He lived at Gunston Hall, near Alexandria. George Washington was inaugurated president of the United States under the new Constitution in the spring of 1789.

As Alexandria enjoyed its forty-year florescence, its political context changed. When Congress decided to build a federal city on land owned partly by Maryland and partly by Virginia, Alexandria was taken from the Commonwealth of Virginia and annexed to the federal district, in pursuance of the Residence Act of 1790. President George Washington had insisted that the new capital be built on his golden road, the Potomac River. He wanted a Paris, on a Potomac Seine, connected to the world by easy sail and enriched by the resources of the Ohio country. In designing the new city, his engineer, Pierre Charles L'Enfant, honored Alexandria and drew it into visual unity with the new capital by proposing a pyramid at Jones Point, to be seen from the president's "palace" and the Mall. Alexandria officially became a part of the District of Columbia on February 27, 1801.

Removed from Virginia and subject directly to Congress in the District of Columbia, Alexandria saw change in the character of its growth. Its new status removed it from the tightening laws of the South pertaining to slavery and free blacks. Thus the city was a relatively secure and comfortable place for free black people to live, and the population of free blacks rose from 52 in 1790 to 836 in 1810. This trend continued for forty-six years, until 1847, when Alexandria left the District of Columbia and returned to Virginia. The free blacks established neighborhoods of their own, including The Bottoms, on the southwest of Old Town; Hayti; Uptown; and Petersburg—today known as The Berg—north of the docks. Alexandria was not without restrictive laws, but it afforded a climate in which free blacks were able to build churches, schools, and other institutions. In a terrible city fire in 1827, black men saved the day by serving as firefighters. Paradoxically, as all this took place, slave markets opened in Alexandria and became major features of the business landscape.

A building, greatly altered today, that housed one of the larger slave markets stands at 1315 Duke Street. In its heyday it was the most successful in town, operated by two Tennessee slavers, Isaac Franklin and John Armfield. Their business extended through the south to Louisiana, where Franklin owned the notorious Angola Plantation, now the site of the Angola Louisiana State Penitentiary. When they opened in Alexandria in 1828, they advertised in the *Alexandria Gazette:* "We wish to purchase one hundred and fifty likely young negroes of both sexes between the ages of eight and twenty-five years." With the plantation culture in Virginia in decline, sales of slaves accompanied the closing of farms. Planters fallen on hard times raised cash by thinning out their slave populations. The market's strategic location made Alexandria a pipeline from old fields to the richer slave markets down south.

*F*ranklin & Armfield's human merchandise, from accounts of the time well fed and clothed, were brought from plantations to the market complex, sold or disbursed for sale there, and herded through the streets to the Alexandria wharves, where they were shipped out in lots by steamboat. Lewis Henry Bailey, taken from his mother as a boy, later remembered the experience of descending the Potomac and sailing the Atlantic around the tip of Florida and over the Gulf of Mexico to the Mississippi River and the final place of sale, Natchez, then his purchase by kind masters from east Texas. He spent years as a house servant and learned to read and write. After emancipation in 1863, he walked back across the war-torn South to Alexandria, where he was reunited with his mother. After he was ordained at the Third Baptist Church in Alexandria, he became a distinguished Baptist preacher.

Although George Washington established the capital city across the river from his hometown, he never lived in Washington. His second term ended in March 1797. Not long after, he made his way homeward to private life, passing through ever more adoring crowds in Alexandria. He lived in retirement a little less than two years and was often in town. The cottage he built in Alexandria stands in replication at 508 Cameron Street. Here his appointments secretary granted and denied interviews, and Washington stayed over when he had dinners and other functions to attend in town.

In the tradition of Europe, the citizens of Alexandria began celebrating their president with a kingly "Birthnight Ball," held on February 22 during his presidency. Candles flickered in every window of every house in town, while torches lighted the streets. The grand upstairs assembly room at Gadsby's Tavern housed the event, and the Birthnight Ball, still a tradition in Alexandria, spawned the national birthday holiday in honor of Washington. Alexandria's eighteenth-century merchants did not fail to make every effort to profit from the dance, one advertising, "For The Birthnight Ball," an array of corsets, "newly improved," the advertiser being "desirous of aiding the Ladies of Alexandria in the best display of their charms."

During the 1790s Alexandria's businessmen, with the world as their field of operation thanks to the river, felt the heat of the conflict between revolutionary France and Britain in constant losses of ships at sea. Although the United States was neutral—and Washington preached against "entangling alliances"—America's shipping was harassed, and its ships were captured at sea in the same vicious international sub-war Patrick O'Brian describes in his sea stories today. Many an Alexandria merchant suffered ruin from the loss of a ship or at least of small cargo aboard someone else's ship. Some hocked furniture or other possessions just to keep their businesses going. The governments of England and France saw the advantage of sanctioning the enterprising private captains, or "privateers," to interrupt the flow of goods from neutrals to their enemies. Local indignation so swelled at this affront to both pocketbook and pride that the militia began drilling in the grassy meadows beyond Christ Church, and citizens gathered at times on Market Square in a warlike spirit.

*E*motions and fortunes rose and fell as France and England continued in greater and lesser degrees their raids at sea. Mariners in Alexandria hesitated in sailing out, lest they be robbed. Sailors feared impressment into a foreign navy, and especially capture by the British, who were likely to bring them to lash or noose as "deserters" on the theory that they had once been British citizens. Nearly all Americans were afraid of a British re-invasion and believed that if Britain's pursuit of Napoleon became a less dominating objective, it might indeed happen.

These issues troubled George Washington in the last months of his life. What proved to be his last Fourth

NATIONAL ARCHIVES (ABOVE); LIBRARY OF CONGRESS (BELOW)

In the 1300 and 1700 blocks of Duke Street were slave "pens," or holding areas, where slaves purchased in Virginia were held until they were shipped down south. Price, Birch & Company, the successor to the more notorious Franklin & Armfield of Tennessee and Louisiana, occupied the house still standing at 1315 Duke (above). The 1836 woodcut (left) shows slaves being marched down Duke Street, probably to the wharves for transit south.

of July and final review of troops took place in Alexandria in 1799. He and friends dined on canvasback duck, hominy, and Madeira at Kemp's Tavern, in the building still standing on the northeast corner of Fairfax and Cameron Streets. After dinner the general walked along Market Square one block up to King Street, where the Independent Blues drilled in his honor.

Five months later, on December 14, he took a chill while inspecting his farm and began to sink. He privately told his body servant, Billy Lee, that this was the end, but he ordered his overseer to bleed him. That night after sunset he died. Dr. William Thornton, learned physician and architect of the

GEORGE WASHINGTON
NATIONAL MASONIC MEMORIAL

This is the clock stopped by attending Dr. Elisha Dick the moment George Washington died; it has not been wound since. The silhouettes of the elder Washingtons were cut by granddaughter Nelly Custis, from shadows made in the firelight.

Alexandrians called down the wrath of their fellow countrymen when, without significant protest, they allowed British invaders to loot the town's warehouses. The political cartoon (opposite) saw wide distribution at the time.

United States Capitol, then being built, heard the news and rushed to the scene with a plan to revive the corpse with lamb's blood and a tracheotomy. Already Joseph and Henry Ingle were finishing the coffin at their cabinetmaking shop on Royal Street. In the banquet room at Mount Vernon Thornton found Washington's body stiff and frozen, on boards that had been laid across sawhorses. The widowed Martha would not hear of Thornton's experiment, insisting that God's will had been done. Washington was sixty-seven.

In Alexandria, church bells tolled for days, as the town joined the nation in profound mourning. Although Washington was buried immediately at Mount Vernon, his town held a ceremonial funeral with official pallbearers. Black crape hung from windows and doors as the long funeral procession threaded snowy streets the general had known so well to the Presbyterian Meeting House in the 300 block of South Fairfax Street.

Why the Presbyterian Meeting House, when Washington was an Episcopalian? Washington's funeral was held at the Presbyterian Church because inclement weather made the streets and sidewalks to Christ Church impassable. Today, if you seek the bronze plaque commemorating the pallbearers, you will not find it at the Meeting House. It is fixed to the western wall of Christ Church, Episcopal.

*A*lexandria greeted the nineteenth century with a mixed attitude. The economy had been severely hit by privateers' attacks on shipping, which continued like a curse through the years of Jefferson's presidency. The town became more populous. More mudflats and marshes, filled, became new streets and lots in what is now Old Town. The economy took a dip in 1807 with Jefferson's Embargo Act, an isolationist reaction to privateering that prohibited American trade with foreign powers. But its own profit making soon filled the gap. Banks opened along Prince and Fairfax Streets, an indicator of one of

Alexandria's occasional high periods. The waterfront was a busy place. Between 1801 and 1815 Alexandria's port carried on an enormous foreign trade: 1,154,778 barrels of flour were shipped out, 323,920 bushels of wheat, 592,054 bushels of corn. Portugal, Spain, the West Indies, and, in large measure, New England were regular customers, the languages of their sailors flavoring the streets, shops, and market.

The capital of the nation proved a rival to the town's development. Banking seemed a new course to survival. When at last the United States went to war with Great Britain in 1812, the banks and the town thrived. Alexandria then had a population of about 8,500, by no means small. Fort Washington, built downriver, purported to protect the capital and, by association, Alexandria. American ships sailed in and out of the port. Warehouses took supplies to store and sell. Yet within two years, the British, having defeated Napoleon and now the most powerful nation on earth, sailed to the United States without hesitation and invaded. Alexandrians saw the sky light up orange on the August night when the Capitol and the White House burned.

Great consternation followed. The commander of Fort Washington blew it up so it would be of no use to the British. Ten days later British Captain James Gordon sailed up the Potomac and captured Alexandria. The enemy remained for five days, and while it was said at the time that the invading troops behaved well, they also looted tobacco, flour, rum, cotton, clothes, and other goods from the warehouses along King Street— warehouses that still stand in use today as shops and restaurants. Alexandria's callers from England cost local merchants about $100,000 in lost merchandise. ■

7. An Answer in Railroads

Alexandria seems by comparison very tranquil today. Fort Washington, in all its magnificence, was rebuilt, largely by a tremendous effort on the part of the free black men of the town. With the end of the war with England—called at the time the Second War for Independence— Alexandrians joined an ebullient nation in an explosive period of expansion in building, invention, and financial schemes involving the vast new lands of the West. The bottom fell out in the panic of 1819. A resulting depression dragged on through the 1820s, and banks failed. Old bank buildings can still be seen: the former Bank of Alexandria, at the corner of Fairfax and Cameron, next to the Carlyle house, and the former Bank of Potomac, now a restored residence, which survived the depression, at 413–415 Prince Street. When prosperity fled, such Alexandria institutions as the Alexandria Academy, which had depended upon it, had to shut down; Washington's endowment had been in bank stock.

Building slowed, but seems never to have stopped. The businessmen put a fair face on the situation. When General Lafayette visited the United States in 1824, he was a guest of the city of Alexandria for several days in October of that year. The tall brick house with the fanlight door at 301 South St. Asaph Street, built

Heroic profiles of Washington and Lafayette as noble Romans in the cause of liberty in France and America

1815–1816, housed him and his extensive entourage. The builder of the house, Thomas Lawrason, had already moved to Louisiana and died, and the house, presumably still furnished and awaiting sale, was loaned from afar to the distinguished guest by his widow. The city built a triumphal arch for the Lafayette parade, featuring garlands of bright leaves and greenery, the noble Frenchman's portrait, and a live eagle, which was provoked to heroic cries and wing spreadings by a boy with a pin.

Soon after Lafayette's visit, another public display was staged in 1825 in a reception for President John Quincy Adams and his cabinet. Crowds came from outside of town, and most of the town turned out for the event, held at Gadsby's, which was by then Clagett's Hotel. The president addressed the Alexandria Library Company, a private organization for the public good that still exists and still owns its books from

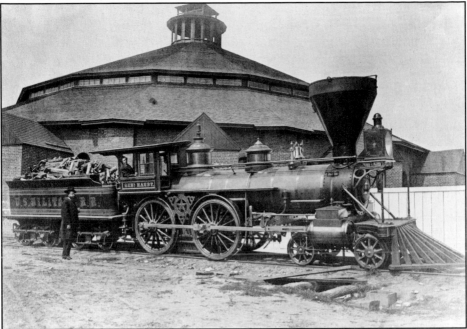

The roundhouse of the Orange & Alexandria Railroad, which stood for many years at Duke and Henry Streets, was built about 1850. During the Civil War, Alexandria was a great railroad center for the Union.

early days, now on exhibit in the Alexandria Library.

It became clear that it would take more than pageants to bring the town back to life. Dreams of the western connection revived in 1830 in the Alexandria Canal Company, which had objectives similar to those of the earlier organization, but now complicated by the silting in of the Potomac. At its destination, Cumberland, Maryland, was the famous narrows, or gap, between the mountains known as the gateway to the West. Work on the Alexandria canal went on for twelve years, with completion in 1843. Alexandria's first tourists appeared in the 1830s. They came by steamboat to see Washington's tomb at Mount Vernon; Alexandria was a stopping place. Regular travelers as well as excursionists stopped here, en route to or from Washington. Several old mansions were adapted to serve the overnight trade.

*O*n March 13, 1847, Alexandria was removed from the District of Columbia and returned to Virginia, and the town had the chance for yet another beginning. The large area retroceded to Virginia as Alexandria County included most of present-day Arlington, although "Alexandria town" (formally a city six years later) eventually became an independent

This sumptuous railroad car, built in Alexandria for President Lincoln, never served him except for his funeral. At left, Abraham Lincoln, 1861

municipality. Several factors influenced Alexandria in pressing for this change. Virginia laws that governed the area had been frozen in 1801 and were archaic and thus limiting. District law denied citizens the vote and forbade the erection of federal buildings in Alexandria. In practice the District system favored the port of Georgetown, which was naturally a subject of continual irritation to Alexandrians.

A rail connection to Alexandria's port seemed the key to the future. Beginning in 1847, freed from the District's regulations, Alexandria entrepreneurs formed one railroad company after another, with little success. After the first train entered Alexandria on the Orange & Alexandria Railroad on May 6, 1851, Alexandria became something of a center, served by several lines. Inventive and desperate Alexandria businessmen convinced four major Pennsylvania coal companies to use Alexandria's port for deposit of the coal and subsequent distribution by boat and rail. Long-vacant warehouses soon brimmed with coal, and coal-piled barges became a common sight on the canal and the river. Sometimes today, in the converted warehouses on lower King Street, one catches a slight whiff of coal. The appearance of cotton factories, shipyards, foundries, and a locomotive works proved that Alexandria was better off in the Commonwealth of Virginia than it had been as a stepchild of the District of Columbia.

*A*nother, implicit reason for returning to Virginia was agitation against the slave trade in the District of Columbia. The selling of human chattels within the shadow of the United States Capitol presented an irony indeed. And as the forces of antislavery began to gather in Washington in increasing numbers, presenting floods of bills to the Congress, their shock over the slave markets turned to a rage of moral indignation. It became clear that the sale of slaves would be prohibited in the District, a measure that was in fact part of the Compromise of 1850. Well before that, Alexandria took steps to protect the "peculiar institution." Retrocession was quick and quiet, but it alarmed the prosperous members of Alexandria's free black community. Now, after half a century, they found themselves trapped under laws of a southern state that restricted free blacks. Many thought it prudent to sell their property and move to Washington. ■

8. Civil War

*V*isitors in the 1850s found Alexandria unpromising. "Alexandria may be said to be a *finished* city," wrote an observer in 1852. "It bears upon it all the marks of decay. . . . There were many residences, but the crumbling wall, the neglected hut, the deserted streets and propped up tenement, spoke eloquently of the absence of enterprise and capital." But an increase in both commercial and residential building in Alexandria suggests economic well-being in the decade before the Civil War. According to an issue of the *Alexandria Gazette* published in the spring of 1854, 700 houses had been built in the city in the preceding three years. Property values nearly doubled.

Soon Alexandria stood once again in the path of major events. The tumultuous polarizing of sectional loyalties in the 1850s climaxed in the secession movement of 1860 and 1861 and the Civil War. The General Assembly of Virginia, sitting at the capital in Richmond, reluctantly seceded from the Union on April 17, 1861, with the proviso that secession be confirmed by public referendum. Alexandria had tended to be unionist in sentiment, but by the day of the vote, May 24, 1861, a large majority voted for secession.

With the withdrawal of Virginia from the Union, Alexandria became the Confederate stronghold closest to Washington. Early conquest was inevitable. Before daylight the morning after the vote, Union troops crossed the river by Long Bridge (approximately where the Fourteenth Street Bridge is today), heading overland for Alexandria. Embarking from the District by steamboat at the same time, a second, smaller company, Union Zouaves, New York Eleventh Regiment, made their way to the port of Alexandria with the plan of joining the other troops at the intersection of Washington and King Streets. Most of the Zouaves had been recruited from among New York volunteer firemen by their commander, twenty-four-year-old Elmer Ellsworth. A flamboyant and ambitious young man, Ellsworth was intimate with the Lincoln family and lived with them in the family quarters of the White House. He longed to be a war hero of the very visible sort. His Zouaves were modeled on the French emperor Louis Napoleon's precision infantry of acrobatic Armenians, complete to *salvar* and turbans. Ellsworth's firemen likewise performed stunning feats in gymnastics, human towers and all. They were bathed in admiration in those first months of the Civil War.

*E*llsworth and the Zouaves landed under protection from the gunboat *Pawnee*, which had been anchored at the foot of Cameron Street for a week, its fierce Dahlgren guns pointed threateningly at the town. Confederate sentries at the foot of Cameron Street fired volleys to warn the troops bivouacked on the other side of town. The streets were otherwise empty. As the day brightened, the Zouaves walked up King Street toward Washington Street. Colonel Ellsworth suddenly spotted something he had set his cap to possess and made an abrupt detour with several of his men. He had seen a very large Confederate flag, flying high atop a hotel; Lincoln had pointed it out to him from his office windows at the White House, and Ellsworth had promised the president he would bring it back.

Since it was well before breakfast time, everyone in the Marshall House Hotel was still in bed when Ellsworth pushed open the front door and started up the stairs to find the flag. Innocence and anger were soon to collide. The hotelkeeper, James W. Jackson, a defiant, headstrong giant who took pride in flying the rebel flag—and his, raised before a cheering throng, was the first to fly over Alexandria—had pledged to kill any man who attempted to tear it down. Wakened by the noise of boots, he slipped out with his shotgun. Ellsworth, now descending, said to his comrades, "Boys, I've got the flag."

Jackson said then, from the shadows: "Yea, and I've got you," and after a scuffle, shot and killed him. His second shot, aimed at Zouave Corporal Francis E. Brownell, missed, and Brownell shot Jackson, killing him instantly. Brownell then took his bayonet and pinned Jackson's corpse to the wooden stairs. Zouaves poured into the hotel, pledging to torch the

When Colonel Elmer Ellsworth (opposite, bottom left), tore the Confederate flag from its staff on the Marshall House Hotel, he was shot dead by hotelkeeper James Jackson (center), who was then shot by Ellsworth's comrade, Union Corporal Francis Brownell, who stands (right) in fame and glory atop the bloody rebel flag. The dramatic scene, capturing the fury of the moment, was painted soon after, from eyewitness accounts.

town in revenge. Commander S. C. Rowan of the *Pawnee* pulled rank and ordered them all back to the steamers, which took them to the middle of the river and dropped anchor for a cooling twenty-four hours.

*E*lmer Ellsworth's remains, returned to the White House with the bloody flag, lay in state with full honors in the East Room. His death was personally devastating for the Lincolns, and the nation joined them in grief for the young hero. Ellsworth was the first Union casualty of note in the Civil War. The wording of the commemorative plaque that marks the site generally comes from the local coroner's report on Jackson's death and preserves the opinion of the incident Alexandrians had at the time, not one shared by Union sympathizers.

Before Ellsworth arrived in Alexandria, Commander Rowan of the *Pawnee* had sent Lieutenant R. B. Lowry to see that the town formally surrendered. The Confederate com-mander, Colonel George H. Terrett of the Sixth Battalion Virginia Volunteers (about half of which was made up of the Alexandria militia companies), refused to surrender but agreed to evacuate. This Lowry accepted, and the Confederates departed Alexandria. It is presumed that they left right away, without goodbyes to their families; those who survived the war would not see Alexandria again for four years.

The city remained in Union hands for the duration of the war. To read the documents of the Union army and the city and memoirs and letters from that time is to see how desperate this period was for Alexandrians. The town was under military control. Oaths of amnesty, renouncing the Confederacy and proclaiming loyalty to the Union, were passed out for Alexandrians to sign. Most refused, and for them the screw tightened. Holding office, taking out a business license, being on the street at night, leaving town, even burying a loved one in a local cemetery required signing the oath. As the war wore on, measures became more severe, even to the point where prominent Alexandrians were made hostages on railroad shipments of Union supplies to keep the Confederates from raiding the trains. "A more forsaken people and desolate city I have never seen," wrote a northern news correspondent, "The houses are low, dirty, and closed; the streets are narrow, filthy, and rough and the people in the sackcloth of sullen humiliation."

*A*lexandria was the first view of the South for many a Union soldier, and its scenes were food for young minds. One Union visitor described Alexandria as "an old-fashioned city of several thousand inhabitants, most of whom were rank secessionists with decided aristocratic and old English tendencies, the very streets resounding with such royal names as King, Prince, Princess. . . ." The presence of several thousand soldiers gave the town a carnival atmosphere. Saloons, in even greater numbers than today, opened along King Street. Women described as dressed "in furs and ostrich feathers" mingled with the soldiers on the streets, and some of the finest houses in town, according to one shocked

*Civil War romance dominates
Alexandria's history and
attracts reenactors like these to Fort
Ward, at 4301 West Braddock Road.
A reproduced main building and
earthworks provide a realistic setting
in which to relive the past.*

Occupying Union troops pose outside the Athenaeum, corner of Prince and Lee Streets. The bearded gentleman seated on the left is Francis H. Pierpont, governor of Virginia as recognized by the Union but not acknowledged by Confederate Virginia.

soldier, shook with "riot and orgie." The scene changed when Union general John P. Slough took charge and order was reestablished. He forbade the sale of liquor and established a curfew. Among his achievements was prohibiting residents from disposing of trash by throwing it in the streets.

Alexandria became a Union hospital, railroad, and supply center. Protected by a ring of forts, the most visible being Fort Ellsworth, on Shuter's Hill, just to the west of where the National Masonic Memorial now

stands, the town became one of the most important facilities of the Union army. Construction of earthworks began the day after Ellsworth's death. Fort Ward, reconstructed meticulously from old documents, has risen again on Braddock Road, representing all the Union forts that once surrounded Alexandria. Groves of trees shade today's picnickers among the embankments, shown in Mathew Brady photographs lined with the structures of war.

The Union army grazed herds of cattle in the hilly meadows that spread beyond the close cluster of the town. About a hundred a day were butchered in a slaughterhouse out King Street, and the meat was packed in salt and dispatched to the front. What was believed to be the largest bakery in the world developed at the corner of Princess and Fayette Streets, producing 90,000 loaves a day. Two hundred employees worked in a sort of assembly line that climaxed at twenty large brick bake ovens and ended at the packing tables. Between 1861 and 1865 the Union supply station at Alexandria distributed 81 million pounds of corn, 412 million pounds each of oats and hay, and 530 million pounds of coal.

*T*he population felt the jolt of great change. An influx of outsiders, all unionists, ultimately included more than seven thousand former slaves. Some eight hundred of these died from disease or the deprivations of being on the road; L'Ouverture Hospital, hastily built, served the sick. The freedmen were called "contraband" by the army, and they found this insulting, especially after the Emancipation Proclamation of 1863. But they seem to have found a place in wartime town life, the majority supporting themselves by taking work on the busy wharves and in the army hospitals, domestic service, and the many new businesses sprouting up in town. Very few took charity. From scraps they built small neighborhoods for quick occupation and surrounded their houses with neat vegetable gardens that elicited universal admiration as well as attracted late-night raids by hungry soldiers.

War business soon boomed.

Alexandria's railroad yard built train cars, including a private car for Lincoln, which was elaborately upholstered and painted. Theaters, stores, hotels, and specialty shops catered to the Union soldiers. What Alexandria had always known as "oyster houses" now appeared as restaurants, places to eat only, with no overnight accommodations. High rents caused practically every household to rent out bedrooms. During the war, army hospitals occupied twenty-six homes and churches, as well as the Episcopal Seminary, around which officers took private villas as residences. The seminary hospital got the best marks from the soldiers, who enjoyed its breakfasts of mutton and potatoes, dinners of beefsteak, tea, and coffee, and its plum pudding at supper.

When Virginia joined the Confederacy, unionists formed the Restored Government of Virginia and fled to what is now West Virginia. When West Virginia seceded from Virginia to become a state in 1863, the Restored Government of Virginia moved its capital to Alexandria. The governor, Francis H. Pierpont, his floating government recognized by Lincoln, lived with his young family in rooms adjacent to the ballroom at Gadsby's Tavern and had his office in the brick building at 415 Prince Street, with its two arched front doors. At the Virginia state constitutional convention, opened by Pierpont in the winter of 1864 at City Hall, Virginia's 1851 constitution was largely reinstated, with an added prohibition of slavery.

Tranquillity was always tenuous in wartime Alexandria. Some eight hundred men had left to fight with the Confederacy. Even before Alexandria

Confederate veterans assemble outside the Confederate veterans' home at 806 Prince Street in 1903, thirty-eight years after the surrender at Appomattox. By then the bloody reality of war had faded into rosy memories of chivalry. Down the street, at the intersection of Washington and Prince, the Confederate soldier in bronze (right), his back to Lincoln's Washington, contemplates the South's surrender and, at his feet every day, rushing rivers of commuting automobiles.

fell, Robert E. Lee had warned his wife at Arlington House to be prepared to flee, which she ultimately did. Most families did not leave. Those remaining, who were longtime Alexandrians, were predominantly Confederate sympathizers. Separation from loved ones in the army and exposure to daily reminders of military rule were an emotional strain. Households experienced financial hardship. Auctions of confiscated property, either taken as spoils or, like the Lees' Arlington House, for nonpayment of taxes, were especially offensive.

*N*ow and then anger built to defiance. The Reverend Kinsey J. Stewart, rector of St. Paul's Episcopal Church, in the 200 block of Pitt Street, omitted the prayer for the president of the United States from the service on a Sunday when Yankee and Confederate peaceably formed the congregation in attendance. Someone spoke out that he should pray for the president; Stewart ignored this, and a group of soldiers pulled him from the pulpit and strong-armed him to jail. General Slough reprimanded the soldiers, but the harm had been done. A mob collected outside the church, and had Slough not sent a heavy guard, there would have been bloodshed. For the balance of the war St. Paul's was to the invaders a symbol of rebel contempt. On one occasion it narrowly escaped being torched.

The news of Lee's surrender at Appomattox brought to Alexandria cheering in the streets and silence behind closed doors. On April 14, 1865, a parade of Union bands and troops fourteen blocks long celebrated the end of the war. That night Lincoln was shot. Alexandrians hid behind lock and key; some houses were searched. Only when the conspirators were apprehended was the grip released. Alexandria's houses were draped in black for the dead president. Troops began to leave. On May 24, Governor Pierpont and his staff boarded the train for Richmond, moving the Virginia government back to its capital. Alexandrians, with the war over, went, first in a trickle, then by the hundreds, to City Hall to sign the oath of amnesty.

The Civil War lingered in the feelings of many in Alexandria for more than a century. After a decade or so of rebuilding, white Alexandria turned nostalgically to memories of the war and the wartime town. When, on May 24, 1889, the Confederate statue was unveiled at the intersection of South Washington and Prince Streets, General Joe Johnson sat on the bunting-draped platform, and General Fitz Lee, then governor, gave the lengthy oration. The statue, titled *Appomattox*, commemorates the sacrifice demanded by war. Through times good and bad it has stood there. Autos have crashed into it; lightning has hit it; political correctness has challenged it. By now it is so familiar a landmark that the street would look strange without it. The ninety-nine names carved on the granite pedestal are those of Alexandrians who gave their lives for the cause of the South. Years after the unveiling, in 1900, another name was added, that of the hotelkeeper James W. Jackson. ■

Eighteenth-century houses and warehouses, relics of prosperity long gone, rot away in the harbor section of an Alexandria worn down by the Civil War.

9. Toughing It Out

*T*he Civil War sharply **increased tourism in Alexandria.** Besides being a southern town that unionists visiting Washington could actually visit, Alexandria was appealing in a patriotic time because of its George Washington associations. Christ Church, where Washington worshiped; Mount Vernon, where he lived; and Gadsby's Tavern, where the Birthnight Balls were danced, attracted thousands of tourists. The former slave market building at 1315 Duke Street was no less a sensation. "Had this slave pen a tongue," wrote one visitor, "what tales it could tell of . . . husbands and wives . . . parents and children, torn from each other's embrace never to meet again on earth."

At the Marshall House visitors took souvenirs to such an extent that by the war's end, little was left of the stairs Elmer Ellsworth had climbed to immortality. Legend and romance grew slowly, like the neglected vines on the colonial brick walls, soon nearly to envelop Alexandria as it slept.

With the Yankees gone and their many facilities broken up and the materials and fixtures auctioned off, Alexandria was sad to see. It had not been burned like Richmond or Atlanta or Columbia, South Carolina, but it had been hard used. Time saw some repair, and life returned to a small-town pace. But Alexandria was poor. Few places in the South struggled as hard to recover. Issue after issue of the venerable *Alexandria Gazette* in the late nineteenth century chronicles unsuccessful attempts, through various business ventures, to regain prosperity.

The port remained in business. If the streets near the waterfront had been in decline before the war, the late nineteenth century saw them begin to crumble. A few barrooms mingled with the sail lofts and marine suppliers along lower King Street; records of police raids and arrests attest that brothels, though ever the targets of public outrage, operated in former residences along the river streets. It is said that the families living on the south side of Captains' Row, in the 100 block of Prince Street, closed their shutters in the evening to shut out noise and disagreeable scenes from the houses across the cobblestones. Nearby, at the corner of Union and Prince Streets, one cold night in January 1869 two residents of the area had a "regular set-to, square up and down, claw and gauge fight." The press reported that "the parties were allowed to keep up the sport until they were satisfied."

A number of docks in existence at that time, all privately maintained and supervised, are now gone. The warehouse area in the blocks near the river was very large, and to our eyes the fine old brick buildings are very handsome. The warehouse to Fitzgerald's Wharf stands at 104 South Union Street, but Merchants' Wharf, Andrew Wales's Wharf, Harper & Watson's Wharf, and Vowell's Wharf have been replaced by the modern waterfront.

Although the railroad became a strong presence, the river still supplied much of Alexandria's lifeblood. From here were shipped the products of the town: bottled and barreled beer, baked goods—tea biscuits sent to England and breads to Baltimore and east—furniture and architectural parts, fertilizers, agricultural products. Old photographs show the waterfront promisingly crowded, but run down from the 1870s and 1880s to its demise in the mid-twentieth century. Mariners were still everywhere every day, making saloonkeeping profitable. Sailors in port liked to steal away and nap in the peace and quiet of the cemeteries, safe from the boatswain's eye. The boats usually departed at night on the quiet river; bells rang on board in measured cadence until they dropped out of sight.

Civic improvements included underground sewers, Alexandria's first. Union soldiers had written home in horror of the "green water" and worse dumped from the houses into open wood, brick, or cobblestone sewers. By the mid-1870s buried terra-cotta pipes transported waste to the Potomac, contributing to the rampant pollution of its water. Many other efforts at sanitation followed, including laws regarding slaughtering animals, the maintenance of livery stables, the disposal of all kinds of waste, and general civic cleanliness. Privies were a feature of houses built as late as the 1890s and were still in evidence in the older parts of Alexandria well into the 1950s.

The steamboat to Mount Vernon stopped in Alexandria for those who wished to look around. Visitors walked up the old cobblestone and brick streets to Christ Church, the Old Presbyterian Meeting House, Braddock House (as John Carlyle's house was called), and Gadsby's

Tavern. Some shops advertised "colonial relics" for sale: old bedsteads, tables, chairs, brass andirons. Certainly some of Alexandria's old houses still contained such things, which found their way into self-proclaimed junk shops. Mrs. Theodore Roosevelt, at the century's turn, liked "antiquing" in Alexandria.

Alexandria struggled to strengthen its economic ties to Washington. The best-laid schemes—usually involving railroads—often failed, not helped at all by the panic of 1893 and the resulting depression, which dashed the town's ambitions for a decade. Both steam and electric railroad companies appeared in and around Alexandria, a few to succeed but most to fail. When recovery seemed near, a second panic came in 1907, and only the intercession of J. P.

Morgan saved the national economy, while, in the South, he swallowed railroads for his huge Southern Railway conglomerate. Other lines, seeing the power and advantages of Morgan's Southern, hurried to link themselves to it. Alexandria was the northern terminus of the Southern Railway. Potomac Yards, north of town, grew into a giant complex.

*E*asy transportation promoted the building of suburbs, greater population, and higher tax revenues. There had been a scattering of suburban settlements through the years, grown up haphazardly, without plans. The new ones were mapped out to the last detail. They began to take form in the 1890s, west and north of town: Del Ray, Braddock Heights, Spring Park, Northridge, the some-

*Fish cleaners on the docks (above) greeted the returning
boats and prepared the day's catch, cleaning and packing in salt for shipment
large numbers of herring, shad, and sturgeon. This scene of about
1890 could as easily have been 1790. Boat building and repair (opposite)
thrived in Alexandria for more than a century.*

what later suburb of Rosemont, spreading over the hills where the Union army had grazed horses and cattle. These represent a full range of late nineteenth- and early twentieth-century architecture. Here and there an early farmhouse nestles up to a concrete sidewalk, its acreage reduced to lot size. A few houses were moved from other places, as is always tempting when the landscape is open and few overhead wires intervene. But most of the houses in these areas were built after the suburbs were established. Today remodeling is almost constant, and vacant lots are practically nonexistent.

A few businesses survived for remarkably long spans. Burke and Herbert Bank still opens its doors today at the corner of King and South Fairfax in a headquarters built in the early twentieth century. Shuman's Bakery, for a century on King Street, now flourishes at 430 South Washington, still making its celebrated jelly cake. Others survive in name. C. C. Smoot & Sons, leather suppliers, which owned tanneries outside the city and kept ware rooms in town, is long gone, but Smoot Lumber Company is still in business, making custom woodwork. Robert Portner's Brewing Company, established during the Union occupation of the town, died with Prohibition, but lives on in the name of the restaurant on St. Asaph Street. In its day Portner's was the largest employer in town. Enterprises of more recent origin were cigar

Morning on Market Square, 1880, from Harper's New Monthly Magazine

factories, glass factories, several chemical laboratories, and furniture manufacturers. All are gone.

*C*ertainly the grandest edifice of the early twentieth century is the George Washington National Masonic Memorial, a reflection of monumental Washington which surveys the town from Shuter's Hill, looking down King Street to the river. Considering the economic context of Alexandria when it was built, it was a project of the most extravagant ambitions. After City Hall burned in 1871, Alexandria's Washington Masonic Lodge No. 22, where George Washington had been Worshipful Master, dreamed of building a fireproof structure for its treasure of George Washington artifacts. Charles H. Callahan took the dream in hand in 1910, purchasing Shuter's Hill, where the ruins of Fort Ellsworth could be traced in earthworks and foundations.

The committee in charge envisioned a national fund-raising program. Seeking a design, they approached the New York architects Helmle and Corbett in 1917. Harvey Corbett, who took the leading role, was later to be one of the architects of Rockefeller Center. He took out his pencil and in a few lines suggested the building you see on Shuter's Hill today. "This is a rough sketch," he told the Masons, "of one of the seven wonders of the ancient world. It is the lighthouse at Alexandria, Egypt . . . erected to guide the ancient mariners safely to shore. What could be more appropriate than a facsimile of that lighthouse in Alexandria, Virginia, on top of the highest hill and overlooking the Potomac?" The Masons adopted the idea and persevered through hard times, war, and depression to design and then build it between 1922 and 1932. Finish work inside ran on until well into the 1960s. "The monument"

Alexandria has always been a town of merchants. On cobblestoned King Street in about 1870, this mercantile house featured tinware, furniture, locks, and rolls of linoleum, together with wagon and buggy parts. A sewing machine is displayed on top of the show window at the left.

is the symbol of the city, linking it to the public architecture of Washington, drawing the eye from almost every point, not the least when you fly into Reagan National Airport from the south and it seems to command everything with a magical presence.

*W*orld War I brought the first real economic upswing to Alexandria. In December 1917, only days after the declaration of war, the United States Shipping Board Emergency Fleet Corporation negotiated with the Virginia Shipbuilding Company and its owner, Groton Iron Works in Connecticut, to build twelve steel ships in Alexandria, each costing over $1.5 million. Hundreds of workers staffed the sprawling shipyard along the waterfront south of downtown. Mrs. Woodrow Wilson christened the first ship, the *Gunston Hall,* on February 23, 1919. Eight more ships followed.

At about the same time, the new Torpedo Factory brought an enormous payroll. Alexandria welcomed it despite its perilous location in the heart of the waterfront. The order for the first of 908 torpedoes to be made there came in the fall of 1919, with delivery in the summer of 1923, well after the war. When the factory closed in 1923, it was a great blow to Alexandria.

The 1920s had not such a golden shine in Alexandria as elsewhere. Although the Masonic Memorial rose on its hill, photographs of the time show an Old Town poor and forgotten. The automobile had ended the need for building houses shoulder to shoulder. Those who could afford to moved to new suburban houses with yards and garages. Economic connections with the federal government in Washington grew ever stronger. The Ford Motor Company built a plant on the river between the shipyard site and downtown Alexandria. Here, convenient to the powers of the capital, Ford's automobiles, trucks, and other products were brought to be shown and sold.

The idea of a parkway connecting Mount Vernon to the national capital, initiated in the 1880s, was realized with the building of the George Washington Parkway in the 1920s. Alexandria's city fathers coaxed its path down Washington Street, right through town, promising to preserve the colonial character of the buildings along the way. Although the promise has been too often broken, bringing the parkway through town was a great coup for Alexandria and one that increased in value to the community over time. Today the parkway is one of the delights of the Alexandria landscape for the views it affords drivers and cyclists.

But the Alexandria streets and buildings George Washington and Colonel Ellsworth had known had sunk sadly into disrepair. When, in 1924, a human fly announced he would perform downtown in Alexandria, great numbers of spectators gathered. First he started up the clock tower on City Hall, only to find it too deteriorated for safety, and had to climb down. A second try at the office of the *Alexandria Gazette* proved impossible for the same reason. The Masonic Memorial being only a stub at that time, the performer finally gave up, leaving behind a disappointed crowd. ∎

*View from an airplane, looking up King Street, c. 1935, showing
the Torpedo Factory on the right, and the waterfront*

10. Old Houses

*T*here is some debate as to
when the world discovered the
charms of Old Town, but there is no
question that Sarah Carlyle Herbert
Hooff, who had a real estate office at
216 Prince Street, was the first activist
in preservation in Alexandria. She
took a proud interest in Alexandria's
old houses and purchased buildings
with the sole objective of assuring
their survival. She resold them as
houses or converted them into rentals,
patching and repairing to extend their
lives a little longer. Others took notice
for business investment. Said one of
her contemporaries, "We'd buy a
house for $300, clean it up and paint it
and sell it for $400." Had Sarah Hooff
not been there to stir interest in the
years around and after World War I,
there might not be an Old Town today.

Alexandria's historic streets greeted the 1920s holding no secrets as to hard times, an embarrassment to local residents. But to outsiders' eyes, the vine-covered brick walls and time-worn doorways were poetic. The house of Dr. James Craik, at 210 Duke Street, photographed in about 1928, was a picturesque reminder of Alexandria's colonial heyday. When New Dealers in the 1930s began buying such old edifices to restore, "Old Town" was born.

A few months before the stock market crash in 1929, two events changed attitudes toward Old Town: a Texas couple restored an old house and Alexandria's American Legion post saved Gadsby's Tavern. Colonel and Mrs. Charles Beaty Moore, enjoying a tour of Virginia, returned from Mount Vernon on a spring afternoon, took a detour through the old cobblestone streets en route back to Washington, and admired the old house at 207 Prince Street. Mrs. Hooff, across the street, encouraged a purchase. Gay Montague Moore, daughter of a former governor of Virginia, determined to make the big brick house beautiful again. She lamented the rotten shutters but was thrilled by the handsome staircase; the plaster walls were soaked with water from the leaky roof and a bathtub on the second floor drained through a pipe poked through the brick wall over the front door, but she was captivated by the fine woodwork.

The Colonial Williamsburg restoration had just begun. Gay Moore called on experts there for advice. Worth Bailey, historical architect, also joined in and became a major influence. When 207 Prince Street was finished, its woodwork polished, its windows curtained in silk, suburban Alexandrians looked on in astonishment at how beautiful a house could be, even "downtown."

The American Legion, Alexandria Post, purchased Gadsby's Tavern about the same time with the good-hearted objective of saving a beloved landmark. Gadsby's was in sad condition. The curators of the American Wing at the Metropolitan Museum of Art in New York had taken the

Sarah Carlyle Herbert Hooff, whose portrait hangs in the hallway of her Seminary Hill home, was the first preservation activist in Alexandria.

ballroom's eighteenth-century woodwork, piece by piece, and reconstructed the room in the museum; they had torn out John Gadsby's mantels and moldings and the elegant Georgian surround of the front doorway. The Legion found money hard to raise, but, with the

support of the community, it suc-
ceeded in one of Alexandria's earliest
preservation triumphs. Gay Moore
went to battle with the Metropolitan
Museum for the return of the architectural parts. She could not get the
ballroom woodwork, but she brought
home the magnificent carved doorway,
which visitors pass through on
entering Gadsby's Tavern today.

In the early 1930s, Congressman
Franklin Korell of Oregon, looking for
housing in the Washington area,
visited Alexandria, where his mother
had been reared. It had an instant
appeal for him. After living in the red
brick house at 312 Queen Street, he
moved on to other houses, ultimately
restoring some six or seven eighteenth-century structures, including
the notable Edmond Jennings Lee
house at 428 North Washington Street.
Like Sarah Hooff and Gay Moore
before him, he provided models. The
first administration of Franklin D.
Roosevelt, meanwhile, had brought
the New Deal, and tens of thousands
of new federal employees swarmed to
Washington. Newcomers who liked
old houses learned that they could buy
one in Alexandria for a very low
price—sometimes under a thousand
dollars—patch it up, wall in the back
yard like a New Orleans garden, and
have a pleasant living situation. The
trip to D.C. on the George Washington
Parkway, opened in 1928, was only
about twenty minutes. And so began
the movement to revive Old Town. ■

Preservationist Gay Montague Moore's portrait still hangs in the Prince Street house she restored 1929–1930.

Entrance hall of the "Georgian Cottage" on Prince Street (opposite), as captured in 1946 by noted photographer Norman Hatch. The random mix of antiques and the fine woodwork painted glossy "colonial white" epitomize Alexandria's earliest residential restorations.

11. World War II

A **transformation in Alexandria followed the outbreak of World War II.** The population in 1940 was 33,523. A thriving Ford plant notwithstanding, Alexandria was a railroad town. On Duke Street were the Mutual Ice Company, a railroad icing station and the largest east of the Mississippi, and the Fruit Growers Express Company, manufacturers of refrigerator cars. Potomac Yards, on the opposite side of town, was soon to become the second largest railroad yard in the world. But in general Alexandria's economy before World War II was far more modest; the

majority of local businesses were small and individually owned. The reopening of the Torpedo Factory in 1937 heralded vast change. By creating several hundred new jobs, it began what would become a population avalanche. As the war approached, the factory's payroll grew. On April 1, 1941, the first MkXIV torpedo was completed and tested at the Piney Point base in Maryland.

*O*n New Year's Day 1942, three weeks after Pearl Harbor, President Roosevelt and Winston Churchill, the British prime minister, attended services at Christ Church. It marked an early recognition of the role Alexandria enjoys today as a symbolic place associated with the Founding Fathers. Although not announced in advance, the presence of Roosevelt and Churchill at George Washington's church was a media event. A regiment of 3,000 army troops patrolled the streets of Old Town. Canvas awnings thrown over the fence at Christ Church screened the visitors from public view. The presidential car entered the church-yard, rolling immediately to the porch on a wooden ramp. Only invited guests within the church got more than a glimpse of the two luminaries, but, reported nationwide, it was a singu-larly touching moment for Americans facing the reality of war.

*T*he population of Alexandria doubled during the war. The number of employees at the Torpedo Factory rose to 6,000. Potomac Yards, expanding furiously, was kept under military guard. A great spillover of new residents from Washington created a demand for more housing than Alexandria could provide. At first the city encouraged homeowners to rent out rooms or partition apartments within their houses. But when the resulting proliferation of apartments seemed to threaten single-family residential districts, a moratorium was set on new one-room apartments. Old Town residents feared rising demand for additions to houses in the historic area, which was the most convenient place for war workers to reside. A board was established to govern alterations to downtown buildings, the first time such a body was constituted in Alexandria. The rationing of food and gasoline intruded on even the simplest lifestyles. Prohibition of pleasure driving in 1942 saw many angry offenders hauled into court. Air

raid drills were held weekly. Lights-out or "brown" nights inhibited even Christmas, and car lights were prohibited on the parkway.

Never in Alexandria's history had there been so much new construc-tion as during the war years. Starting especially in 1943, with the first federal financing, the suburbs began to grow. Funded by the Reconstruction Finance Corporation at a cost of $40 million, Parkfairfax and Fairlington Village, begun in 1943, offered town house living in a landscaped setting. Some five thousand units made the two combined the largest housing development in the nation; 85 percent of the occupants were government workers. Tax-conscious city fathers were disappointed that Fairlington, though on land always considered part of Alexandria, was actually in Arling-ton County.

*A*t the same time, Chinquapin Village accommodated 350 families in low-cost housing, and a mobile home park, intended to be temporary, served a similar purpose in Del Ray. The government condemned two acres bounded by Patrick, Madison, First, and Alfred Streets for apartment buildings restricted to African American tenants. Well-made structures of two stories, the James Bland Housing Project was set in trees and lawn, its scale suggesting the early row houses of Alexandria. This development was contemporary with a similar building program of low, slate-roofed houses on Princess Street, in the neighborhood mentioned earlier as The Berg.

Not a single turkey could be found in Alexandria for Thanksgiving

1944. Gasoline shortages made stalled and towed cars a familiar sight. Coal, the principal heating fuel, was in such shortage by 1945 that protestors picketed the home of John L. Lewis, president of the United Mine Workers, at 614 Oronoco Street (today known as the Lee-Fendall house). People roughed it through the cold weather without heating systems, but fireplaces being common, smoke from wood fires spiced the air. In the spring each year of the war, the town and its suburbs had turned-up earth everywhere for victory gardens. A city law was passed making it a felony to rob them—a protection not offered for such gardens during the Civil War.

On May 8, 1945, Germany surrendered. While all of Washington danced in the streets, Alexandria is remembered as quiet. Everyone went to church. Alexandria's twenty-six churches were packed with worshipers. In May a special V E (Victory in Europe) ceremony convened on Washington Street before the Confederate statue. Five thousand Alexandrians had gone to war. One hundred thirty five died. General Carl Spaatz, of 206 Duke Street, commander of the Eighth Air Force, which was the muscle of the main air offensive against Germany, was greeted by a cheering crowd of Alexandria neighbors. To them he said: "It's a wonderful feeling to come back to a community that wasn't destroyed by the war. It's our job to see that it isn't destroyed." Victory in Japan brought thousands into the streets in a festive mood. "Many girls were kissed on King Street," noted the newspaper. "Colored paper adorned wires, poles, and store fronts." ∎

12. Old Town as a Symbol

*P*ostwar Alexandria, now **more than doubled to a town of 67,000, reacted with horror when the closing of the Torpedo Factory was announced in 1946.** Politicians gathered to negotiate. The government had no further use for a torpedo manufactory. The factory was converted to dead storage, and the hive of workers went elsewhere. When the Nazi archives crossed the ocean they were brought to this vast, abandoned space, hundreds of drab filing cabinets lined up, making long corridors lighted by single lightbulbs dangling from wires. Here, among hundreds of thousands of Nazi manuscripts, were stored Hitler's personal papers, including Eva Braun's photo albums. In tomblike silence the papers remained there for thirty years, until removal to the National Archives annex in Suitland, Maryland.

Both Old Town and the suburbs grew. Big government was now a way of life, with legions of employees working for it and related businesses. A procession of new residents, often temporary, moved to Alexandria. It became clear that the new epoch was to be based not in industry but in real estate and office jobs. Alexandria's conversion to this new economy was slow relative to that of many other cities in the postwar years, but steady.

Social changes, which so often seemed to pass over Alexandria, sometimes made themselves felt.

Alexandria's civil rights movement came early. The town's large and venerable community of African Americans had pushed for civil rights in the past. In the 1880s a delegation of black Alexandrians had called on President Grover Cleveland at the White House, asking that an African American be appointed postmaster at Alexandria. The president took it under consideration, but politics prevented favorable action. Race relations in Alexandria had been stormy. The newspapers record a conflict in 1853 between blacks and whites with sticks, stones, and pistols. Beatings and murders with racial overtones took place in both the nineteenth and early twentieth centuries. In the nineteenth century, a lynching of a black man took place from a lamppost in front of the Ramsay house, at the corner of King and Fairfax. Not long after, a black man was dragged from his home and killed with an axe, then set afire behind the Carlyle house, and no arrests were made.

BLACK HISTORY RESOURCE CENTER

*B*y 1939, well before the issue of civil rights was in the national spotlight, pressures to integrate public facilities had taken expression in a sit-in at the Alexandria Public Library on Queen Street. The event was one of the first civil rights sit-ins in American history and a harbinger of peaceful protests throughout the nation. Relative peace accompanied the integration of Alexandria's public schools in the 1960s.

Some brought in the new, while others sought new means of keeping the old—or, at least, the appearance of

the old. In 1946 residents of Old Town, fearing that success would spoil the quaint atmosphere they loved, developed rules that governed architectural change to historic houses. One of the first such laws in the United States, after those passed in New Orleans and Charleston, on which Alexandria's regulations were based, the Alexandria Historic Ordinance, with modifications, has shaped the development of Old Town ever since. Interpreted by the Board of Architectural Review, a city-appointed volunteer board, the regulations are brought to bear on any changes within what is called the Old and Historic District.

The strength of the 1946 regulations was severely tested in the 1960s when federally funded urban renewal undertook the remaking of the central city. The heart of the city's downtown, as it had been inherited from earlier generations, consisted of buildings from all the periods since the mid-eighteenth century. This heart was cut out and replaced with a spare architecture, suggesting the lines of

Peaceful protesters (opposite), left to right, William Evans, Otto Tucker, Edward Gaddis, Morris Murray, and Clarence Strange, are arrested at the Queen Street Library, 1939. One of the nation's earliest "sit-ins," the event resulted in no charges.

Alexandria's identity as a town lies in its wealth of old and historic buildings. Some have been lost. This one, which faced Market Square, might have been saved by today's protective laws.

the oldest buildings but in a modern vernacular in common use across the nation at the time in shopping centers and industrial buildings.

The Historic Ordinance controlled alteration to a building but could not prevent demolition. Preservationists fought many battles to save old buildings that fell to the wrecking ball. Some 40 percent of Old Town was lost to a commercial image that, it was believed, would attract business. Within the central core, major landmarks were preserved—Gadsby's Tavern, John Carlyle's house, William Ramsay's house, City Hall—and in the residential neighborhoods that spread out from Market Square, little was changed. The powerful sweep of urban renewal, however, transformed the urban character of Alexandria from that of an independent city to that of a suburban town, reflecting its relationship to Washington.

Over time the Historic Ordinance has been strengthened. Today no building can be demolished without the city's approval. Buildings are saved and reused today which would

never have been considered for preservation in the past. The Torpedo Factory, for example, is now a major arts and crafts center. The idea in the 1970s of local preservationist Marian Van Landingham, it has gained worldwide praise and has been a prototype for many such conversions. To the Old Town historic district has been added the Parker Gray area, northwest of Old Town, a late nineteenth- and twentieth-century neighborhood governed by an innovative set of rules uniquely tailored to maintain its essential character.

Alexandria has been active in encouraging property owners to grant scenic easements on historic structures and open land. In donating an easement to some agency—usually partly to the public, through the Alexandria Historic Resources and Preservation Commission, and partly to the private, nonprofit Historic Alexandria Foundation—the property owner forfeits the rights of future alteration and development, say, of the exterior, or even portions of the interior, of the house. The restriction then applies to the property, presumably in perpetuity. Such restrictions entail the property, and the owner can expect lower property taxes. Both the Lafayette and the Dulaney houses, across Duke Street from each other at the St. Asaph intersection, are under scenic easements.

The town's outer borders expanded. When it was returned to the Commonwealth of Virginia in 1847, Alexandria had been county seat of a much larger Alexandria County. In 1870 it became an independent city— an oddity in the United States—and in 1920 Alexandria County became Arlington County. Alexandria did not remain small, however. Since its founding in 1749, it has expanded eight times, twice in the eighteenth century, twice in the nineteenth century, and through four major episodes in the twentieth. Those of 1915 and 1930 took in Rosemont, George Washington Park, Town of Potomac, Del Ray, Northridge, and the surrounding neighborhoods, a wise move on the part of the city fathers to acquire the prosperous suburbs as taxpayers. By far the largest extension of the town, however, was the last one, in 1952, the vast area out Duke Street to the west of Old Town, called the West End, annexed from Fairfax County. Today the town of Alexandria covers 9,994.6 acres, or 15.661 square miles. Most of this contains development of one sort or another, primarily residential. It represents one of the densest concentrations of population in the United States.

In the 1970s, Alexandria entered another building boom that carried it into the twenty-first century. If one counts remodeling and additions to houses, it affected every area of the town. New subdivisions filled former woods and fields. Vacant lots in Old Town saw new construction in the old style. Filled land along the river, where the shipyard and the Ford plant once were, is now thickly planted with new and expensive town houses. They often sell before the roofs are complete; some are sold in multiples to a buyer who combines two or three into one. The West End development began slowly, with some large apartment houses and commercial warehouse areas, as well as shopping centers. In the late 1990s it swelled into immense apartment blocks, town houses, and development of all sorts, until, at this writing, about half of Alexandria's residents live in the West End.

Alexandria is more than ever a prime location for business and businesspeople needing to be in fairly close proximity to Washington. More room, a more favorable physical context in which to live and do business, brings hundreds of businesses to Alexandria, notably lobbying and special interest firms and high-tech organizations. Being "inside the Beltway" around Washington, Alexandria has the cachet of a good location for government-related work. A rapid turnover of houses and apartments suggests the ups and downs of both politics and federal contracts. In spite of all else, however, tourism, firmly rooted in the romantic appeal of historic buildings, remains Alexandria's most important and enduring economic staple.

The Metrorail system links

A Christmas parade revives Alexandria's Scottish heritage, attracting merrymakers from everywhere.

American cities today.

Miraculously the essence of the town has survived. On a map of the entire city, Old Town is a tiny place. The street down which a young George Washington led his militia toward the Ohio country is a little thread that goes westward and keeps going and going into areas that bear little resemblance to the Alexandria of the historic imagination. Alexandria is home to a wide range of people generally still united by the original fascination of the place: business. In the flood of population and growth, Alexandria has been able to keep its image as a town, defined symbolically by the river village where it began, Old Town. ■

Alexandria to Washington, and automobile access is, for the time, easy. Dulles and Reagan National, two great airports, provide access to the world. Wise city planning, anticipating these years of intense development, has defined commercial and residential areas, allowing for a mix in some places—as has always existed in Alexandria—but preventing the unbridled sprawl typical outside many

Alexandria offers a variety of activities for visitors.
Not least are long walks down historic streets and along the
Potomac's edge. Here strollers, following the
river path in a "new town" section north of Old Town,
look across the river at Washington.

II   All Around Alexandria

The city has many neighborhoods and communities, with names both old and new. Beyond Old Town, historic buildings and sites are scattered through the newer suburbs. It would take a book much greater in length to cover everything in Alexandria that attracts the eye. The emphasis here is Old Town.

The tour is organized as follows: the waterfront; King Street (east to west); streets parallel to King, in sequence south from King and then north from King (west to east); and cross streets (north to south). It concludes with the Alexandria suburbs and the George Washington National Masonic Memorial. Site numbers appear in red and relate to the maps.

There are two maps at the back of the book: Sites 1–51 are shown on the fold-out map of Old Town Alexandria; sites A–C are shown on the City of Alexandria map on pages 142–143. After the heading for each street are listed the names of their individual sites.

*Today Old Town celebrates
a vigorous economic revival while
maintaining the mix of
residential and commercial life that
has characterized it since
the city was laid out in
the mid-eighteenth century.*

Old Town

*T*his area, now well into its
third century, is the original city.
Architecturally rooted in the eighteenth century, it presents a variety of
building styles. Most of the notable
activity of the city's long history took
place in this part of town. Pre-
automobile, the houses of Old Town
were built close together in tight rows,
making the distances between things
shorter. The interesting mix of

building uses, while representing
fewer contrasts today than 200 years
ago, still says much about the social
makeup of early Alexandria. Planters,
merchants, seamen, bakers, rope
makers, teachers, preachers, slave
blacksmiths, cooks, free black
teachers—the whole spectrum of early
American society created the buildings that now make up Old Town,
clustered first by the river.

The Waterfront

King Street starts at the waterfront on
the Potomac River. Most visitors enter
Alexandria today from the land side,
either by car on Washington Street, six
blocks west of the river, or from the
King Street Metro station, sixteen
blocks west. Not so in early times,
before railroads superseded shipping
and sailing ships and steamers still

77

*The Potomac River,
originally Alexandria's reason for
being, is again one of the town's main
assets. Docks once crowded with
riverboats and seagoing
ships now largely serve sailors on
pleasure craft, droves of
artists, and fishermen relaxing
from the work week.*

*Lower King Street, showing Fitzgerald's Warehouses, at right, during
a flood in the early twentieth century. Alexandria has known the river's anger
from time to time, when the ice melts far upstream, and new threats come every
few years. The ferry terminal at the end of the street is now gone.*

WILLIAM FRANCIS SMITH COLLECTION

brought cargoes and passengers from the rest of the world to the Alexandria docks. The Potomac rises in the Appalachian highlands of western Maryland and West Virginia. Alexandria is about halfway along the river's course to Chesapeake Bay. The Potomac is a fine river, easy to fall in love with, and Alexandria encourages that. Waterfront parks allow for pleasant riverside walks on grassy paths and wooden docks and provide places to sit and enjoy the scene.

The waterfront lost its original look of a working seaport long ago, but elements have been preserved, with new construction kept to the older scale and surviving buildings put to new uses.

Market Square and Environs (Sites 1–5)

Two blocks up King Street, going west from the river, are some of the finest surviving eighteenth- and early nineteenth-century warehouses in the United States, most built on filled land when the riverbank was extended after the Revolution. Especially notable are **Fitzgerald's Warehouses (1)**, on the southeast corner of King and Union Streets. Alexandria merchants filled their warehouses with flour, salt, rope, tar, preserved food, and military supplies and realized great profit in the French and Indian War and the American Revolution; during the War of 1812, however, the invading British

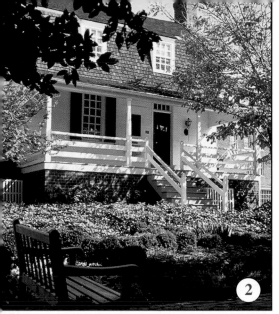

*Drawing room of a private house
overlooking King Street*

demanded tribute from the warehouses. Fine merchant residences also face lower King Street. Bernard Chequire, an emigré from revolutionary France, built number 202 about 1795, and Colonel George Gilpin built number 206 at about the same time, both with counting rooms (offices) or shops on the street floors. Also of historical interest in this area is the Corn Exchange, at 100 King Street, a fine Italianate commercial structure built as an agricultural clearinghouse about 1871.

At the top of the hill at Fairfax Street, King Street is flanked by two symbols of Alexandria's historic commitment to business: on the north stands the **Ramsay house (2)**, a reconstruction of a house built by merchant William Ramsay, an eighteenth-century Dutch-gable structure, the original of which was one of Alexandria's earliest buildings. It is now Old Town's tourist information center. On the south, **Burke and Herbert Bank (3)** occupies early twentieth-century neoclassical headquarters. Established in 1852, it is one of the oldest banking institutions in the United States.

King Street runs along the south end of **Market Square (4)**, an open plaza very different in appearance today from the cluster of shingle-roofed shanties in this location that were the city market of old times. Few places in the nation, however, are more cherished in historic memory than this. From here George Washington marched his men off to the French and Indian War; soldiers left from and returned here in the Mexican War; both Confederate and Yankee rallies took place on the square. It was the town meeting place as it is today. On the south, a mix of old and new buildings includes the early nine-teenth-century Mason Building, at the corner of King and South Fairfax Streets, built by George Mason's heirs, and brick and wood replacements, made during urban renewal, of older structures. The big building on the north is **City Hall (5)**, its bland neo-Williamsburg "rear" facade added forty years ago. You will want to go around to the opposite side, on

Cameron Street, to see the distinctive 1873 front, an architectural reflection in brick of Napoleon III's New Louvre in Paris, and to Royal Street to see the tower, reproduced from the original after the fire that destroyed City Hall in 1871.

Nearby but discussed in sequence below are two Alexandria landmarks: Gadsby's Tavern (**40**), across Royal Street from the tower side of City Hall, and the John Carlyle house (**44**).

King Street West of Market Square (Site 6)

West of Market Square, King Street crosses Washington Street, the other axis of the town, which leads north into Washington, D.C., and south to Mount Vernon. Along King, on the approach to this juncture, is the densest area of 1960s and 1970s urban

Entertainer and shoppers on Market Square

renewal in Alexandria. The buildings, generally of light brick, follow a quasi-historical American vernacular popular at the time. Some replace important early structures, an example of rehabilitation gone to excess but a part of the Alexandria landscape today. The site of the **Marshall House (6)**, scene of Colonel Elmer Ellsworth's fatal confrontation with the Confederate hotelkeeper James Jackson, is at the corner of King and Pitt Streets. When Nathaniel Hawthorne visited during the Civil War, he found the stairs and other elements associated with the event already cut away by souvenir hunters, so little of historical significance was left when the hotel burned down in 1872. Visitors can read the commemorative bronze

plaque on the Holiday Inn, which now stands on the site. Today, the mix of old and new on upper King Street has charming scale and, weathered a bit through some decades, pleases the eye, particularly at dusk, in the shadows of its trees, when daylight is fading and the night lights rise.

Crossing Washington Street and continuing west, the George Washington Masonic Memorial, discussed in sequence at the end of the tour **(51)**, looms in the distance. Along the ten blocks of King Street that terminate the Old Town area, all the way to the Metro station and the Masonic Memorial, is a happy mix of restaurants and antiques and collectibles shops, many with apartments above. Buildings of architectural quality

The long stretch of King Street from the river to the George Washington National Masonic Memorial (opposite) passes restaurants (above) and shops, both on King proper and on side streets (below).

stand alongside others of no importance other than being where they are, making a beguiling, human-scale shopping area that rivals in popularity the earlier, better-known blocks of lower King Street.

Streets South of King Street East to West

Prince Street (Sites 7–9)

The streets parallel to King Street and the cross streets are a largely residential part of Alexandria's grid. Prince Street south of King extends from the commercial high-rise district near the Metro station to the river. Beginning away from the river, in the 1200 block of Prince, the row houses create a closed streetscape, varying from small wooden tenement, or rental, houses of the 1880s and early 1900s to much earlier buildings. Of note is 1113 Prince, built in 1816, a handsome house in the Federal style, so described for its slight departures from Alexandria's eighteenth-century norm: larger windows and loftier proportions, the touch of neoclassicism in the transom, and columned mantels inside. Yet it is as simple as can be, in the Alexandria tradition. Across the street, at 1112 and 1114, are less ambitious neoclassical houses with panels inset in the brick between the first and second floors, giving a quaint monumentality to two ordinary houses of 1818.

The pattern of small brick houses continues down Prince. Double houses at 915 and 917, with the oriel windows protruding from the second floor, were designed by Glenn Brown, Alexandria's noted architect. Watch Old Town streets for the occasional big arch, all of them echoes of the popularity of Richardsonian Romanesque in the late nineteenth and early twentieth centuries.

Twin Federal houses at 817 and 819 Prince Street, built around 1803, are a variation of the Alexandria form in their trimness and scale. Tucked away in this block, which they share with houses of many periods, they are highly enriched with bracketed cornices and plastered arches over the windows. Rear additions diminish the splendid proportions of the main blocks. Trimmings of stone from the Aquia Creek quarry adorn 806 Prince,

a mansion built Savannah style for the Reverend James T. Johnston, rector of St. Paul's Church in the 1850s. He had moved by the time the Union confiscated the house for a hospital. After the war it became a home for Confederate veterans, then headquarters of the United Daughters of the Confederacy, who open it occasionally today as a museum.

The handsome house at 811 Prince, with its long front stairs, was built in the 1850s of brick and stone and once included the adjacent iron-fenced garden, where wounded Yankees took their leisure and enjoyed flowers and an iron fountain. An opulent house by Alexandria

Old buildings such as these late eighteenth- and early nineteenth-century row houses on Cameron Street (opposite) and Prince Street (above) often housed both residence and shop or office.

standards, 811 reminds one of old houses in Brooklyn Heights. The interior is elaborately finished in cast plaster ornamentation. The wooden section on the east side was originally a conservatory. William Reardon built the house next door, at 805, with its timidly Richardsonian arch, in 1895. Fine, Flemish bond brick walls and Federal trim in wood combine in the 1808 house, sensitively restored, at 808 Prince. Two excellent Federal houses that terminate the block were built about 1818.

In the 700 block, two houses draw attention. On the south, at 706 Prince, is the Daingerfield house, a large building that grew in several episodes, beginning about 1803 as a substantial row house built by Thomas Swann, with side hall and circular staircase, probably much like the Lafayette house (**38**). A wing was added to the west about 1840, and, at

that time or a little later, a long wing to the east. During the 1860s or 1870s, monumental woodwork detailing and a mansard roof brought the mansion into step with the French Second Empire style. In 1905, when the house became a convent, the Sisters of the Holy Cross remodeled yet again to serve St. Mary's Academy, and later for residences for nurses. Today it is subdivided into condominiums.

On the south side of the street, at number 711, the William Fowle house, long known quaintly as the "Georgian Cottage," is an early building skillfully remodeled to represent the New England Federal style of architect Charles Bulfinch. An actual period version of the type is at 607 Cameron Street (**20**). Very likely the core of the Fowle house was originally the two-story rear wing of a vanished house oriented to Washington Street, which

ERECTED
TO THE MEMORY OF THE
CONFEDERATE DEAD
OF ALEXANDRIA VA.
BY THEIR
SURVIVING COMRADES.
MAY 24TH 1889

THIS MONUMENT MARKS THE SPOT FROM
WHICH THE ALEXANDRIA TROOPS LEFT TO
JOIN THE CONFEDERATE FORCES.
MAY 24, 1861

(8)

the property once faced. Beginning in the 1890s, the house underwent drastic changes, and by the turn of the century, with the third floor added, it looked as it does today. The "Georgian Cottage" may have been the work of the architect Glenn Brown, well-known colonial revivalist, who practiced here at that time and restored the interior of Christ Church in 1893.

At the intersection of Prince and Washington Streets stands the **Confederate statue** (7) on a high granite pedestal. Sculpted by Caspar Buberl after a painting by John A. Elder of Richmond and titled *Appomattox*, it shows a contemplative young soldier on the day of surrender. The most frequently noted thing about it is that the figure faces south, turning its back on Washington.

The remaining blocks of Prince Street are rich in early architecture. The tall brick building at Washington and Prince is the former George Mason Hotel, now offices, but the best accommodations Alexandria had to offer from the 1920s through the 1960s. The pair of houses on the north side, at 605 and 607, were built in the 1850s under one ownership, the smaller being a residence for the children and their governess. Their Italianate detailing in wood is set off by stucco walls scored to resemble blocks of stone ashlar. Take note of the 1890s Richardsonian remodeling of the old church building on the corner of Prince and St. Asaph; look in the alley on its left and note the pilastered wall, remains of the original Greek Revival church, probably designed by Robert Mills, architect of the U.S. Treasury and other federal buildings.

Patrick Murray built the frame cottage at 517 sometime after 1775. Mounted atop an "English," or raised, basement, it originally had front steps to the street; when city fathers in the 1790s decreed unobstructed side-walks, the front door had to be closed, the steps removed, and the entrance moved to the side. The house has had almost no exterior alteration since. The eighteenth-century brick house across the street, at 520, long divided into two separate residences, was built by prominent biscuit bakers. In the 1830s Horatio Clagett made it a hotel specializing in overnights for river visitors to Mount Vernon.

The buildings at 413–415 Prince Street were built in 1804, in the Federal style, as the **Bank of Potomac** (8). Here, during the Civil War, the

Restored Government of Virginia, recognized by Lincoln, kept headquarters, awaiting the fall of Richmond and ascendancy to power.

A mingling of late eighteenth-century houses with early nineteenth-century Federal and 1850s Greek Revival buildings characterizes the 200 and 300 blocks of Prince. Number 216 Prince, completed about 1815, was the office of Sarah Hooff, pioneer preservationist of Old Town, and 207 Prince was a seminal restoration carried out by Gay Montague Moore in 1929 that turned public opinion toward preserving Old Town.

A massive Doric portico fronts the **Athenaeum (9)**, at 201 Prince, built to house the Old Dominion Bank in 1851 and later a library and a church. The design comes from carpentry pattern books of the time for designs in the Greek Revival style. Orange was the base color of an original marblelike paint treatment of the building, much like that on Arlington House. Today the Athenaeum is the gallery of the Northern Virginia Fine Arts Association.

Colonel Robert Townshend Hooe, first mayor of Alexandria, built the tall, Dutch-roof house on the opposite corner, at 200 Prince, about 1780, and after his death it became a bank. A very fine house indeed, it was fully paneled, but in the twentieth century the interiors fell victim to raids by decorative arts museums seeking old rooms in which to display collections of antiques. The Georgian interiors, rendered in painted pine, are in the St. Louis Museum of Art. The house is now divided into several houses. Painting and some altered detailing detract from the excellence of its

facades on Prince and Lee Streets. The handsomest staircase in Old Town survives in the rear portion of the house, connecting the second floor with the third, remnant of the elaborate woodwork once in the house.

Captains' Row, the 100 block of Prince, provides Alexandria's classic romantic image of the past. Most of the row houses date from the late 1820s, replacing earlier houses lost in the terrible city fire of 1827, but they follow older forms. For most of their early lives, these houses were immediately adjacent to the busy wharves; hence their associations with mariners. Prominent entrepreneur Captain John Harper built many of these and other houses on Prince Street on speculation. The cobblestones, retained here and on Princess Street, were once common on the ways and alleys of Alexandria and still lie beneath modern pavements.

Duke Street (Sites 10–15)

Beginning in the 1700 block of Duke Street is the **Slave Trade District (10)** of early Alexandria. Joseph Bruin's "Negro jail," a holding center for slaves, occupied the two-story brick house at 1707 Duke Street from 1844 until the Civil War. The building now houses the Charles R. Hooff real estate company. In the next block, at 1401 Duke, standing with dignity and remarkable irony is Shiloh Baptist Church, established in the neighborhood of the old slave markets by freedmen in 1865, the last year of the Civil War. One block east, at number 1315, is the surviving part of Franklin & Armfield's slave market, which also seems to have been less a selling place than what was called a "slave pen" for

holding what slave owners and traders viewed as human chattels until they could be dispatched by steamboat to the markets in New Orleans and Natchez. Slaves were sometimes marched cross-country as well. This building was originally only two stories and had a walled yard with ranges of rooms. With Christ Church and Gadsby's Tavern, it was a major tourist attraction during the Civil War and also served as a hoosegow for misbehaving soldiers, for whom the

Two youthful Alexandrians cool off, c. 1900, at one of the public water pumps installed in the eighteenth century and still in use more than a century later.

Heavy snow on South St. Asaph Street, c. 1917, with Buster Brown right on the mark. Note the "flounder" house across the street, the rear wing built first, of a house never realized. Such wings can be found behind most early Alexandria houses.

iron bars were added.

Between the two slavery sites, at 1123 Duke, is a fine house that gives a good idea of what much of Old Town was like before the 1970s restoration. One of the best early structures in town, built about 1810, it had grounds that covered a picket-enclosed quarter block, with outbuildings and an orchard, and was for years the residence of George Mason's heirs.

Farther east on Duke Street are nineteenth-century row houses here and there, but the street does not become solidly lined until the 800 block and from there to the river is largely residential. Number 806 was the home of William Dulaney, Theodore Roosevelt's barber. Notable in the 700 block is the **Caleb Hallowell School (11)**, a large yellow house with a rooftop lantern that actually faces Columbus Street. Built in the 1820s, it became a military school in 1888, with Caleb Hallowell as master. He and his uncle, Benjamin, were leading educators of early Alexandria. The

Hallowell School is restored today as condominiums.

The **Benjamin Dulaney house** (**12**), 601 Duke Street, with its side garden and stable, is one of the finest houses in Alexandria. Benjamin Dulaney married Elizabeth French, who had been George Washington's ward, and George and Martha Washington dined here as family in the years after the Revolution. The richly paneled interiors and handsome open staircase have been almost untouched since the house was built in the early 1780s. The rear service wing probably dates from the late 1820s. On the high front steps, General Lafayette addressed the multitudes on his visit in 1825. He occupied the Lafayette house, at 301 South St. Asaph (**38**), but found its steps less a stage.

Farther along Duke Street are rows of fine Alexandria houses that present an architectural delight in wood and brick. Notable are number 521, built in the 1790s, with a magnificent, fully paneled room across the second-floor front. The Alexandria style of Flemish bond brick and wood trim is in full development here. The old houses have built-up paint; corners once sharp are rounded by time. Roofs, originally wood shingles or slate, have since the 1850s been more typically of tin, painted or, much later, tarred in an effort to make them last longer cheaply.

The three houses at 414–418

James Craik, c. 1760

Duke show the Alexandria adaptation of the Greek Revival style. Heavy pilasters and entablatures frame the entrance doors, and hoods crown the first-floor windows. The English basements sometimes contained kitchens. These houses featured brick privies in the small backyards. In the next block, number 500 is such a Greek Revival house Victorianized with the addition of a mansard roof and dormers and the sunny bay window so popular in the late nineteenth century. Number 501, across the street, is an early house once occupied by George Washington's private secretary Tobias Lear and his wife Fanny, who, at least once in the autumn of 1795, entertained George and Martha here at dinner.

The **Dr. Elisha Cullen Dick house (13)**, at 408 Duke Street, bears the name of the colonial physician who occasionally ministered to George Washington and his slaves. Summoned to the dying hero's bedside in 1799, Dick tried to stop a too-enthusiastic bleeding of the patient, begun on Washington's own orders. It was too late. To record the final moment, the doctor (one assumes lacking a pencil) stopped the hands on a nearby clock. That clock, which can be seen today in the museum at the George Washington National Masonic Memorial, has never been reactivated. From 1900 until her death here in 1925 the Dick house was the residence of the philanthropist, physician, and pioneer social worker Kate Waller Barrett, in her time Alexandria's most famous citizen. Her portrait can be seen in the Queen Street Library **(24)**. Next door at 404, on the corner of Duke and Pitt, is a tall house of 1808, remodeled in the Greek Revival mode and occupied in the 1850s by Benjamin H. Lambert, pioneer colleague of British medical scientist Joseph Lister. Dr. Barrett purchased it early in the twentieth century for the Florence Crittenden Home for unwed mothers.

At 210 Duke is the **Dr. James Craik house (14)**, home of Washington's comrade in the French and Indian War and later surgeon general of the Revolutionary army. Among the finest eighteenth-century houses in Alexandria, the Craik house has two entrances, one into the house and the other an alleyway leading beneath the house to the rear yard. A grand drawing room extended the full width of the second floor.

At 202, 205, and 207 Duke Street are "flounder" houses, really the rear wings of houses for which the front blocks were never built. The name is unique to Alexandria, although the custom of building such wings was common enough in early American

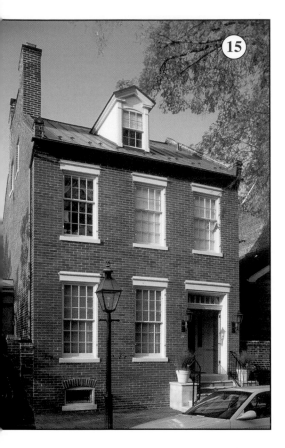

Wolfe Street (Site 16)

The 800 block of Wolfe Street is a mingling of rehabilitated nineteenth-century row houses and new houses built in the old style. Of interest is the tall corner house at 827, which looks so much like an inn that it is usually called "the inn," but until recent years was a rental house. Number 708 Wolfe, a freestanding house with thick walls of brick covered with clapboards, dates from the late eighteenth century, and much of its large lot is still intact. Holland House, at 415 Wolfe, is a rambling structure behind high brick walls, a combination of houses from just after the American Revolution and a large, fine garden. Through the iron gate on Wolfe Street note the ancient sycamore tree, which rivals that at the Presbyterian Meeting House school, around the corner on South Pitt Street.

The **Alexandria Academy (16)** is set back on the right in the 600 block. The academy, finished in 1783, was privately endowed, and George Washington himself established a fund for "poor boys and girls." Robert E. Lee was a student there. Midway in its long life it was a school for free blacks, and it was used by the Alexandria public school system until 1966. The academy has been restored by the Historic Alexandria Foundation and is in use as a computer school for children. Next door is the venerable Alexandria Little Theater, which has a regular and popular season of plays each year. Performances originally were held in the ballroom at Gadsby's Tavern. The wrought iron fencing is from the United States Capitol, sold as surplus about 1851, when the Capitol's

cities. "Flounder" simply means that no windows faced the neighbor's yard; hence the windows, like the "eyes" of a flounder, were on one side. Number 206, the **General Carl A. Spaatz house (15)**, was the wartime home of the unassuming General "Tooey" Spaatz, brilliant commander of the Eighth Air Force, centerpiece of the Allies' air offensive against Germany. He commanded the air assault on Japan, which culminated in dropping the atomic bomb. His report on the Blitz in 1940 pointed out weaknesses in the Luftwaffe and strengths in the RAF and helped convince President Roosevelt that England, with U.S. help, could survive.

Alexandria Academy was funded privately in 1785, and in 1887 became the city school. Pupils (below) in 1917 proudly display birdhouses they have made.

new iron dome was being built.

Francis and Sarah Smith built the freestanding brick mansion at 510 Wolfe, probably the largest of all Alexandria's historic houses, in 1854. Italianate in style, it rides on a deep cellar with brick arches. The last few blocks to the river are mostly lined with small row houses, many of them wooden, as most early Alexandria buildings were. Each has its small rear garden, typically paved with bricks and planted in azalea, holly, and boxwood.

Wilkes Street (Site 17)

At Wilkes and Royal Streets is a remnant of the Civil War period, a **railroad tunnel (17)** built between 1851 and 1855 to bring trains underground to the docks. It now stands unused, but it saw great activity well into the mid-twentieth century. The Burke Mansion, at number 210, is the most important historic building on Wilkes Street, although the street is lined with old and new row houses, some of the former greatly remodeled. Built soon after 1810, the Burke Mansion, a freestanding house in a belated Georgian style, dominated the entire block with gardens and stables. The property is much subdivided

today, and many of the surrounding houses are not as old as they appear.

Streets North of King Street, East to West

Cameron Street (Sites 18–23)

The "castle" house at number 913 was made up in the late 1820s from several existing houses brought together and united by the old architectural trick of adding a built-up parapet to give verticality. At number 912 is the **Charles Bennett house (18)**. Bennett, the Alexandria contractor who rebuilt the White House after the British burned it, built this house for his business partner, later bought it, and died there in 1839. Going

Light Horse Harry Lee, c. 1809

against traffic, Cameron Street passes the north side of Christ Church, which is discussed later in sequence (32), and doglegs to become two-way in the 600 block, where the architecture represents a mix of styles. The **General Henry "Light Horse Harry" Lee house (19)**, at number 611, was occupied in 1810–1811 by the famous Revolutionary War cavalryman and his family, including his three-year-old son, Robert Edward, before the family relocated to Oronoco Street, to a house discussed on that part of the tour. A big risk taker and a dreamer, Lee was perilously close to financial ruin when he moved here from Stratford Hall, in Westmoreland County, Virginia, where Robert E. was born.

The finest of Alexandria's Federal houses is the **Lord Fairfax house (20)** at number 607, built by a New Englander who imported the "Bulfinch Regency" style prevailing there. For all the grandeur of its facade, it is not a large house, but seems to have been built in the manner of an English "casino" or French *pavillon*, as a secondary house for entertaining. Its interior splendors defy Alexandria's "Presbyterian" simplicity, with elaborate composition cornices and a spectacular circular stair that rises two floors to a skylight. A succession of Lords Fairfax, British peers who somehow retained their vast land holdings in Virginia after the Revolution and were related to the

20

The Lord Fairfax House, 607 Cameron Street, was more "modern" when built than any other Alexandria dwelling of its time. It features the architectural bravado of a deep niche that pierces the crisply rendered facade of Flemish bond brickwork. The interior (opposite) is embellished with neoclassical ornament; architectural conservation is seen in process on the "geometrical" staircase (left) that winds two full stories.

Fairfaxes of Belvoir Plantation, lived there for about thirty years in the nineteenth century, renting nearby 208 Royal Street for extra room.

Number 602 Cameron, opposite and second in from the corner of St. Asaph Street, was probably built in the 1820s and is best known as the Alexandria residence of the novelist

Frances Parkinson Keyes, whose books *Joy Street*, *Crescent Carnival*, and dozens of others were bestsellers from the 1930s through the 1960s. Before leaving Alexandria for New Orleans in the 1950s, she was active in community affairs, attracting much national interest to Alexandria, as well as such famous friends as Franklin and Eleanor Roosevelt, Perle Mesta, Alfred Lunt, and Lynn Fontanne. Her picket-enclosed rose garden stood where the hulky adjacent structure has been built since her time.

The wooden cottage at 508, atop a stone basement, replicates **George Washington's town house (21)**, the original of which, built in 1769, was demolished in 1855. City Hall's principal facade (**5**) commands the entire south side of the 300 block. Cameron Street on the north side, facing City Hall, presents a remarkable row of early buildings, originally retail stores, as they are today, with residential quarters above and small walled gardens behind. Notable buildings here are number 311, built before 1817, with its courtyard and porches, and number 305, once **Duvall's Tavern (22)**, where George Washington was entertained on New Year's Eve 1783. In the next block, biscuit baker and minor real estate magnate Henry Nicholson built number 211 in 1805 in classic Alexandria Federal form.

The 100 block is flanked by new construction that followed the last major phase in the redevelopment of Old Town under urban renewal. On the south is **Cameron Mews (23)**, town houses built in the late 1960s facing a central court and among the best built and most architecturally compatible of all the earlier residential developments in Old Town. On the north side, replacing wartime warehouses, is a condominium development built in the 1980s that suggests the Queen Anne style of Victorian London. Elmer Ellsworth and his men landed at wharves which once stood at the foot of this street.

Queen Street (Sites 24–25)

Queen Street Library (24), at number 717, was Alexandria's first permanent city library, opened on August 20, 1937. Named for Kate Waller Barrett, whose house is on Duke Street (**13**), the library has been remodeled, preserving the original facade of the 1930s. The public library system in Alexandria has grown enormously and has built a new central library on Duke Street near Landmark. Queen Street's Barrett Branch is now an annex, serving as a library, but also containing extensive collections on Virginia history and genealogy, which attract researchers from all over the world. This building, in 1939, was the scene of one of the first peaceful civil rights demonstrations in the nation.

Number 603, an academy in the 1850s, is now condominiums. Interesting and varied row houses complete the blocks of Queen Street to Founders' Park, on the riverbank. Highlights are later houses, such as 317 and the towering pair at 504 and

*President George
Washington, 1795*

GEORGE WASHINGTON'S MOUNT VERNON,
BENSON J. LOSSING, 1870

506, all built in the palmy period of the 1850s. Number 312 is a fine Federal building, the **Admiral William F. Halsey house (25)**, owned by the rugged and pugnacious "Bull" Halsey, commander of major sea operations in the South Pacific during World War II. On his flagship, *Missouri*, the official surrender took place on September 2, 1945. A perennial favorite is the little mansarded house at 418, perhaps built in the 1870s or 1880s to reflect the French design of the new City Hall.

the blocks nearing the river. The rear
wing of the house on the north side,
with its large garden, was built in 1800
by Charles Lee, attorney general of the
United States (1795–1801) and later a
distinguished attorney figuring in the
defense of individuals associated with
the alleged treason of Vice President
Aaron Burr. President John Adams
visited Lee here in 1800 and admired
beautiful plantings of clover and
timothy in the garden.

Oronoco Street (Site 26)

The **Robert E. Lee Boyhood Home**
(26), at 607 Oronoco, was for years a
house museum. George Washington
was entertained here by the builder,
John Potts, Jr., who completed the
house in 1795, and by the subsequent
owner in 1799, William Fitzhugh, who
loaned or rented the house to Light
Horse Harry Lee, gallant veteran of the
Revolutionary War. Fallen on hard
times, Lee occupied other houses in
Alexandria, but this became the home
where he lived with his second wife,
Ann Carter Lee, and their brood,
including young Robert E. Lee. Soon
after moving here, Light Horse Harry,
beaten nearly to death in a political
incident in Baltimore, went to the West
Indies to restore his health and died,
leaving a widow with lots of land but
no money. Denial and hard work saw

Princess Street

The gray-painted brick house at 711
was once a side-hall row house, built
in the late 1790s. Gardner L. Boothe
completely remodeled it in 1913–
1914, moving the front to the street
and doubling the size, transforming it
into a classic Colonial Revival form.
This and 711 Prince Street are
Alexandria's finest Neo-Colonial
houses of the type, both remodelings
at times when Alexandria people took
great pride in their colonial history.

The 600 block of Princess retains
its cobblestones, beginning an
interesting neighborhood of old and
new, notably in recent construction in

Robert E. Lee, 1831

THE ALEXANDRIA LIBRARY,
SPECIAL COLLECTIONS

the Lees through. Here Lafayette called on the widow of his old comrade in 1824. Robert E. Lee applied for admission to West Point from this house in 1824, beginning a military career in the shadows of his famous father and emerging at last to achieve his own fame in the Civil War. The Boyhood Home, open to the public, was built as a twin to the adjoining house at 609, which was occupied by various Lees in the early nineteenth century. In the winter of 2000 it was sold as a private home, sparking a national controversy.

Old Town North to South

King Street divides the following streets north to south, as reflected in

Louis Hicks, director, gives instruction in the Black History Resource Center, which features African American history and genealogy.

two sets of identical numbering.

Alfred Street (Sites 27–30)

The **Black History Resource Center** (**27**), at 638 North Alfred Street, is a fascinating stop. A library and

Firefighters (above), c. 1900, outside the Columbia Firehouse, 109 South St. Asaph Street, now a restaurant. Friendship Firehouse (right) contains original equipment and is open to the public.

archives, it sponsors exhibitions and programs on African American history, especially in Alexandria. At 322 North Alfred is Meade Memorial Episcopal Church, founded and built in 1873 by the vestry of Christ Church for its black members. The expansion, one of the best in Old Town, was made in 1990. Note the original bell in a separate tower. **Mechanics' Hall (28)**, at 114 North Alfred Street, built in 1818, housed an association of builders; it is one of Alexandria's most important original buildings in the Federal style, Victorianized with various additions, including the bay window in the original front door. Number 110, a fine late-century exterior of glossy red brick with a prominent bow, was built in 1893; it is offices today, with a wing added on the north side.

Friendship Firehouse (29), built in 1855 as headquarters of a volunteer company founded in 1774, is at 107 South Alfred. The firehouse is

maintained as a museum. Don't miss the ancient fire engine and fire memorabilia from two centuries. At 219 South Alfred Street is a notable Victorian house, a romantic ensemble of copper oriel window and great Richardsonian arch. On the corner of South Alfred and Duke Streets is the venerable **Alfred Street Baptist Church (30)**, which began as an African American congregation in 1803. Today the vast membership has expanded into a lofty new church, but the early church, with its classic Alexandria red-painted brick walls, has been preserved. Music at Sunday services here is memorable.

South beyond the Alfred Street Baptist Church, a mix of restored and new houses and compatible public housing covers an area that was virtually abandoned as recently as the 1970s.

Columbus Street (Sites 31–32)

The churchlike structure at 211 North

Columbus Street was **Potomac Lodge No. 8 (31)**, International Order of Odd Fellows, acquired by the organization in 1841 and remodeled in the 1880s. It incorporates walls from the earlier Female Lancasterian School, one of two in town in the early nineteenth century, operated according to a regimented system by which students took part in teaching. A Union prison occupied it during the Civil War. This was where ration tickets were distributed during World War II. Today number 211 is condominiums.

The 1960s houses at 206 and 214 are preservationist William J. Murtagh's enlightened solution to a bank's need for a parking lot in an old residential neighborhood: new houses built along the street with a parking court through an archway to the rear. Across the street is Christ Church Row, a series of matching houses built in the early 1870s over part of the graveyard of Christ Church, which extended north two blocks. Newspaper accounts from the time tell how bones turned up when the cellars were dug. At 202 and 204 are the "twin sisters," two Victorian houses built alike in the 1880s.

In the 100 block of North Columbus is one of the city's architectural jewels, **Christ Church (32)**, built in 1773. Spend some time here and savor one of the best eighteenth-century buildings surviving in the United States. The few alterations are those of affectionate use through time. Brick laid in Flemish bond combines with corner and door trimmings of sandstone quarried downriver at Aquia— painted, as this stone always was in the eighteenth century. The building was designed from English architectural pattern books of the day, notably William Salmon's *The London Art of Building* (1748) and Batty Langley's *The City and Country Builder's and Workman's Treasury of Designs* (1756), also apparently used by Washington at Mount Vernon. Regularly scheduled tours tell the many stories associated with the church. Take special note of the obelisk in the churchyard, paid for by

The grounds of Christ Church serve as a city park.

the city and designed by Robert Mills in memory of Alexandria contractor Charles Bennett. At 111 South Columbus Street is a house constructed by Bennett in 1810 and Victorianized in the 1870s by the addition of cast iron window hoods.

The annex buildings adjacent to the church are not without interest. Parish Hall, facing Columbus, was built in the late 1850s in the mildly Neo-Gothic "Army Corps of Engineers style," which makes one suspect the hand of one of the vestrymen at the time, Robert E. Lee, a member of the corps. The other parish building, facing Washington Street and the churchyard, built in the 1950s by architect Milton Grigg, makes a fine partnership with the rest of the complex. Across Columbus Street from Christ Church are row houses built in the mid-1990s, carefully mindful that they make an appropriate setting for the church.

Washington Street (Sites 33–37)

Today the main thoroughfare of the town, this street was a post–Revolution addition to Alexandria's plan, as its name implies. Since opening in 1932, the George Washington Parkway has given it dual service. The tall, painted brick landmark with the lantern on top, at 515 North Washington Street, is the **Old Cotton Factory** (**33**), the first historic site one sees on entering Alexandria from the parkway. It was built in 1847 as the Mount Vernon Cotton Manufactory, for the weaving of cotton cloth. The Union army silenced the looms to make it a prison, which became one of the most notoriously cruel prisons of the Civil War. It became a spark plug factory and has since been apartments and is now offices.

Lee Corner greets one at the intersection of North Washington and Oronoco. It is so named for the early occupants of the houses that face it. The late eighteenth-century house at 428 North Washington Street was owned by Edmund Jennings Lee, a prominent local citizen. Restored in

Alexandria's romantic walled gardens began to appear in the early restoration period of the 1930s, replacing chicken yards and outbuildings.

34

the mid-1930s by Congressman Franklin Korell of Oregon, it was one of several restorations he undertook in the interest of helping revive Old Town. The **Lee-Fendall house (34)**, the rambling wooden house at 614 Oronoco Street, is a mid-nineteenth-century house inside of which is buried an earlier house of 1785. Widow Elizabeth Steptoe Lee, former mistress of Stratford Hall, and her second husband, Philip Fendall, give the house its double name. In the twentieth century it was a home of John L. Lewis, an extraordinary man who worked his way up from coal miner to president of the United Mine Workers Union. A stormy public figure inside and outside the labor movement, he maintained a devoted following from labor throughout his long career. He kept his famous collection of antique silver in the Lee-Fendall house but usually resided in

Washington. The house is open to the public.

Number 329 North Washington, a house very little changed in more than a century, was built in the 1820s, with the third story added perhaps in the next decade. William Gregory, merchant from Kilmarnoch, Scotland, had an American outlet in Alexandria for carpets and woolen products from his family's factory. The arched red brick house at 417 North Washington, built about 1890, is an especially fine rendition of Richardsonian Romanesque. Numbers 307, 305, 303, and 301 were simple wooden buildings with brick "flounders," built in 1853 as rental dwellings and remaining in the same family ownership until 1925. They were architecturally embellished in the 1930s, but their transformation is sensitive, and they present a proud front to Alexandria's main street.

Number 220 North Washington, the **Lloyd house (35)**, was built in 1797 by the tavern owner John Wise, and is a superb example of the eighteenth-century Alexandria style at its most formal. Note the handsome Flemish bond brickwork and the remarkable carved wooden doorway, the whole frontispiece seemingly held up on two small marble brackets below. The history of this house is intimately tied to that of Alexandria, not the least during the Civil War, when Yankee soldiers appeared early in the morning after Lincoln's assassination, ordering that black crape be hung from the windows. After many episodes of peril, the house was at last rescued and acquired by the city for restoration.

Number 131 North Washington Street, across from Christ Church, is a large, yellow-painted brick house, probably built in 1820 by early

Alexandria mayor Christopher Neale. With architectural transformation in 1870, probably by the architect Nathan Starkwether, designer of the Episcopal Seminary (see the section on Seminary Hill), Dr. Montague M. Lewis created the French Second Empire house of today.

Washington Street Methodist Church (36), at 115 North Washington Street, is an old congregation, the Methodist Episcopal Church South. Methodist Episcopal Church North moved to the Northridge suburb, transporting its brick building to the new location. Washington Street Methodist's Victorian Gothic facade covered an 1851 Greek Revival front in 1899, retaining the rich red paint once very popular on brick buildings in Alexandria.

The large brick building on the northeast corner of Washington and King (629 King Street) is all that remains of four more or less identical structures that defined this intersection in the early nineteenth century. The remaining house has long been given over to commercial uses, although it remains intact on its upper floors. During the War of 1812 it was the residence of Brigadier General Robert Young of the District of Columbia Militia. On the corner of Washington and Prince Streets is the U.S. Post Office, completed during the Depression and later converted into a federal court building. Held in the glare of extensive press coverage, the building has witnessed some notorious federal spy trials in recent years.

The **Alexandria Lyceum (37)**, at 201 South Washington, today the city's history museum, was built in 1839 as a subscription library and lecture hall. Greek Revival portico and pilasters, walls of plaster scored to represent ashlar stone blocks, and earthy coloration distinguish this hall, where John Quincy Adams, Caleb Cushing, and other luminaries addressed Alexandria's citizens. The library held over 4,000 books. After some years as a library, it was sold for use as a house. General Fitzhugh Lee (1835–1905), colorful officer of the Confederacy in the Civil War and of the U.S. Army in the Spanish-American War and governor of Virginia, married Ellen Bernard Fowle of Alexandria here in 1871, at a ceremony attended by celebrities of the former Confederacy. The poet Archibald MacLeish (1892–1982) lived here in the 1930s, when the interior had been remodeled in a Mount Vernon manner. Restored today to its configuration as a lyceum, it is once again a popular gathering place for exhibitions, lectures, meetings, and music.

The Downtown Baptist Church, originally the First Baptist Church, 212 South Washington Street, originated on this spot as a meetinghouse in 1805. After the early building burned, it was replaced in 1830, and the present Gothic Revival church was built, incorporating these brick walls, in 1858–1859. First Baptist moved to the suburbs in 1954, and a contingency of members stayed in Old Town to serve the city population. Adjacent to the church, going south, is Lloyd's Row, which extends to Duke Street. With one exception, only the facades survive. Built around 1811–1815, they were fine Federal houses, large of window and elegant of finish. Judge William Cranch, Abigail Adams's

37

nephew and one of President John Adams's "midnight appointments," acquired number 220, as did, years later, colorful, courageous R. W. Avery, General George Pickett's courier, at the storied charge in the battle of Gettysburg.

In the 400 block of South Washington, west side (numbers 401–413), is a delightful row of wooden row houses with pocket gardens behind, all restored as shops. Built in the 1840s, they were typical of many frame houses in Alexandria, now gone. The Queen Anne French-Lawler house, at 517 South Washington Street, is an unusual house for Old Town, both because it is an ample, freestanding house and because its Victorian assuredness survived the colonial craze, when such architecture was unfashionable.

North St. Asaph offers a mix of old buildings and many new ones, with some adaptations. The old city jail of the 1820s, the only Alexandria building designed by Charles Bulfinch, survives only as a facade in the 200 block of North St. Asaph, east side, screening new town houses built behind it.

Columbia Engine House No. 4, at 109 South St. Asaph, serves today as a restaurant and bar. The 200 block has handsome houses from the full run of years, from the late eighteenth century (520 Prince Street) to the early 1900s (219 South St. Asaph). Number 209 is a fine Greek Revival house, little changed, with its original gas chandeliers in place. The gas fixtures at number 212, across the street, still function.

The **Lafayette house (38)**, 301 South St. Asaph, served as quarters for General Lafayette and his suite, including his companion Fanny Wright and her sister Camilla, when they were in Alexandria in 1824, on his flamboyant tour as Hero of Two Worlds. It is a beautiful house, ample of spaces, superbly finished. Note the front door surround with its carved wooden stars.

Number 305, built about the time of the Lafayette house by Benjamin Shreve, is notable for its simple rendition of the Alexandria house form. It was owned by the Stabler family of the Apothecary Shop (**45**). It appears not much changed externally, while 307, adjacent, has obvious alterations and is about the same age. In this block, at numbers 317 and 321, are two "flounder" houses—without windows on one side—the latter built in the late 1820s, about two decades after the first.

Pitt Street (Site 39)

On North Pitt Street is the same mix of old and new row houses that characterizes parts of St. Asaph, North Alfred, Lee, Royal, and Queen Streets. The median date of the older houses is about 1850. They embody the traditional Alexandria house form, almost to the house. Exceptions are 204, 206, and 208 North Pitt, built in the 1850s, which are more like Baltimore houses than Alexandria examples of the time. Number 212 is a remarkably handsome house, set atop a high English basement. The freestanding house at 213, built in 1823, like 305 South St. Asaph, figures in the story of the Stabler family.

St. Paul's Church (39), on the east side of the 200 block, Gothic Revival in style, was developed from plans by Benjamin Henry Latrobe,

39

40

Gadsby's Tavern, Alexandria's noted eighteenth-century hotel, lives again as a city-owned museum. Three centuries of dancers have celebrated Washington's birthday at an annual Birthnight Ball on the polished floor of Gadsby's upstairs ballroom.

architect of the Capitol when the church was begun in 1817. The interior is as dramatic a bit of carpentry as can be found. During the Civil War, St. Paul's was considered a rebel nest. The rector was dragged from the pulpit for refusing to mention Lincoln in his prayers. Rowdy soldiers more than once threatened to burn it down, and, but for the cooler heads of their superiors, might well have done so.

Royal Street (Sites 40–41)

Harlow Row, 202, 204, and 296 North Royal, named for the contractors John and George Harlow, who built the three houses in 1874, forms a delightful Victorian ensemble, although with minor alterations. The Fairfax peers rented number 208 as supplementary space for their home around the corner. Numbers 219 and 221, built by James McGuire in the early 1830s, show how the Alexandria taste prevailed long after the eighteenth century, and these are especially fine and restrained examples.

At 134 North Royal (corner of North Royal and Cameron Streets) is celebrated **Gadsby's Tavern (40)**. Externally it is clearly two buildings, that on the left may be as early as 1770, and the one on the right was completed in 1792. Here the Founding Fathers wined and dined, and here Washington's birthday is still celebrated with the Birthnight Ball. Around the side, on Cameron Street, are the remains of the original underground icehouse, unearthed by the city's archaeology department during restoration in 1976. The rear wing along Cameron is retained for the use of the American Legion, which rescued the building from destruction

long before anyone else paid much attention to Old Town. The grand edifice opened its doors again to celebrate the nation's bicentennial, and you will enjoy dining there and exploring Gadsby's, attic to cellar.

Number 112 South Royal was the home and shop of Joseph and Henry Ingle, cabinetmakers, who made coffins for both George and Martha Washington and furniture for Thomas Jefferson. Number 122 is an eighteenth-century house with Neo-Colonial alterations to the doorway. The row at 214–216 were built sometime after 1815 as rentals, in Alexandria's lucrative market. Number 220, built between 1829 and 1832, is a sophisticated Federal house, although the lower windows were extended at a later time. Certainly among the most charming of Alexandria's old houses is 317 South Royal, which, although probably built in the 1840s, lingers in the eighteenth-century wooden vernacular. **St. Mary's Catholic Church (41)**, established 1795, completed on this site a magnificent, tall-spired Gothic Revival church in 1857. In 1895 it was remodeled into the quarry-faced stone structure of today, incorporating all but the external features of the old building.

Fairfax Street (Sites 42–47)

The **Jonah Thompson house (42)**, at 211 North Fairfax, built 1800–1805, emerged from a quarrel between Thompson and the architect Benjamin Henry Latrobe. How much of Latrobe is in the result is uncertain, for, being an advocate of plain classicism, he would have sniffed at the fancy Anglo-Palladian touches. It was a vast couple

*Flower garden behind
the Carlyle house*

of houses, with vaulted rooms and odd stair halls, reminding one of old merchant houses in parts of London. Today it is condominiums, with the interior's once sumptuous cast plaster ornamentation torn away. Allow yourself a walk down the alley to see the marvelous loggia at the rear, a flamboyant oddity among Alexandria's conservative old buildings.

At number 201 is **Lyle's Tavern (43)**, now offices and apartments. It was known as Kemp's Tavern when George Washington met here with the Potomac Canal Company. A succession of well-known people kept this tavern, with its comfortable accommodations, large stables, and kitchen with hot-water boilers for cooking and bathwater. In 1798 the people of Alexandria gathered here to honor Secretary of State John Marshall, later chief justice. At number 121, facing

Market Square, is the eighteenth-century **Carlyle house (44)**, home of the prominent early merchant, which is open for tours. On the southeast corner of Fairfax and Cameron is the former Bank of Alexandria, chartered 1792 and built 1803–1807, which

Apothecary Shop exterior, late 1860's (left)

lasted out the bitter 1820s but went out of business in 1834.

The **Stabler-Leadbeater Apothecary Shop (45)**, at 105–107 South Fairfax, is one of the most complete early drugstores anywhere, filled with original materials used over nearly 150 years. Such an array of bottles of strange liquids, boxes of powders, and other mysterious ingredients you will find nowhere else. Patrons seeking relief from ailments included Martha Washington, Robert E. Lee, and other Alexandrians down to 1933. In the mid-nineteenth century **Green's Steam Furniture Manufactory (46)**, at the corner of South Fairfax and Prince, produced a large line of "sets" or single items in Victorian cottage styles. At 212 South Fairfax, the home and shop completed by 1786 by Dr. William Brown, physician general of the Continental army, is distinguished by fine, early timber frame construction. The brick kitchen at the rear retains its huge fireplace and an iron roaster.

In the 300 block of South Fairfax, on the west side, is the **Presbyterian Meeting House (47)**, a splendid brick church built in the 1830s after the original eighteenth-century structure burned. It is in the best New England meetinghouse style of master builder and architectural author Asher Benjamin, with the best of building materials and construction, not least being fine brickwork, ironwork, and carpentry. It incorporates some walls from the original church. The sanctuary, with its basilican colonnades, was once heated by iron stoves sunk in the niches along the walls. The great concave niche behind the pulpit was designed to project sound. George Washington's official Alexandria funeral was held in the building replaced by this one. The Tomb of the

Advertisement for Green's in the
Alexandria Gazette, *1846*

Unknown Soldier of the American
Revolution is in the graveyard behind
the church.

Lee Street

South Lee Street presents town
houses similar in style but with
enough variety to make this an
interesting stretch. Most are from the
nineteenth century, a few from the
eighteenth, and some of later date but
remodeled to look older than they are.
The last are usually easily identified.
Number 106 is especially interesting.
It apparently began life as a warehouse and was then a commercial
bakery, an armory, and a business
until it became a residence in the
1930s. One of the most spectacular
blocks in town is 500 South Lee,
where a row of houses along the west
side of the street overlooks Lee Street
Park from a ridge and has a panoramic view of the river. This is a
good destination for an evening walk,
for the night lights are beautiful.
Two blocks away, at 714 South Lee
Street, Zion Baptist Church provides
a delight to the eye in a diminutive
Gothic Revival building that edges

the street on its upper floor and falls
down the hill below. It was established
in 1864 by freedmen, its location
perhaps determined by the shipyard,
which then sprawled between here
and the river.

Union Street (Site 48)

On Union Street north and south, at
the foot of King and Prince Streets,
are warehouses of mellow brick that
date from the eighteenth century to the
1850s, intermingled with modern
buildings, also of brick, intended to
blend with the old. Captain John
Harper's warehouse, built about 1785,
now shops, stands on the northwest
corner of Union and Prince Streets; on
the southwest corner is a similar
warehouse which has been converted
into a residence.

The 100 block of North Union
Street features the **Torpedo Factory**
(**48**), Alexandria's arts center, where
working artists pursue their crafts and
sell works from their studios. With a
history stretching back to World War I,
the Torpedo Factory seemed to offer
nothing to a renovated Alexandria and
was scheduled to be demolished.

The Torpedo Factory, once declared a useless relic, now houses many professional artists as well as the superb Alexandria Archaeology Museum.

Citizen pressures overwhelmed the planners, and you see the happy result. South from there on Union Street, early warehouses mix with new construction, until South Union yields to new town house developments. On the way, on the river side is the enormous complex of Interarmco, supplier of firearms. Riverside walks provide the opportunity to view pleasure boats, especially on weekends, and occasionally larger ships, which are usually either cruise liners bound to or returning from the Caribbean or freighters carrying newsprint for the *Washington Post.* ■

Alexandria Neighborhoods

(Sites **49–51** on the Old Town map; sites A–C on the City of Alexandria map)

Neighborhoods in Alexandria are little principalities within the larger kingdom, each with its own character and pursuits.

At the gateway to the **Alexandria suburbs** are the George Washington National Masonic Memorial, discussed at the end of the tour, and two railroad depots, **Union Station (49)**, built in 1905, which faces the memorial across Callahan Drive, and the 1980s **King Street Metro station (50)**, which faces town at a confluence of major thoroughfares. From here four streets lead to important suburban neighborhoods: King Street to Henry Street and to Parker Gray; Commonwealth Avenue, to Del Ray; Russell Road, through Rosemont to Northridge; and King Street, extending beyond Old Town to Seminary Hill and the surrounding suburbs. Braddock Road, which runs between Northridge and

Mount Vernon Avenue, in the popular Del Ray neighborhood, was born anew in the 1990s with shops, restaurants, and lively evening entertainment.

the earlier Del Ray and Rosemont sections, was the old Leesburg Pike, along which Braddock and Washington marched to the west. One of Braddock's original cannon is mounted at the intersection of Braddock and Russell Roads

The Parker Gray District

Adjacent to and slightly northwest of Old Town, this city neighborhood, like Old Town, is under laws to preserve its character. Here, however, the approach is different: not to alter or remodel toward some historical theme, but to preserve the twentieth-century mixed character of the area as it is today. Where an Old Town resident might, for example, be required to use wooden shutters mounted on hinges in the early manner, a Parker Gray resident might be permitted to nail shutters directly to the wall; aluminum siding, taboo in Old Town, might be allowed here. The vernacular of the district has been taken as the rule book. Preservationists all over the nation are watching Parker Gray with interest. How successful the approach will be remains to be seen, but since controls were enacted in 1989, the district has avoided some of the intrusions universally regretted in Old Town. The name Parker Gray came from the high school that once stood in its midst.

Del Ray

Commuter rail service to Washington gave rise to Alexandria's first suburbs in the late nineteenth century. Trains made the commute to D.C. until they were replaced by buses in 1932. Two residential areas, Del Ray and Mount Jefferson, were established in 1894, northwest of the city, within the township, the Town of Potomac, and the development of St. Elmo soon followed. St. Elmo's promoters offered buyers one year's free commute to Washington by train. Efforts to keep the three developments under one township culminated in a charter in 1908, but the town was defunct by 1929, leaving the area part of Alexandria.

In this highly popular residential

Alexandria's early twentieth-century neighborhoods have a wealth of houses in the bungalow style, which, at the beginning of the twenty-first century, is probably the most popular American old house form. These, each with its yard and big trees, line a street in Rosemont.

area, all generally known today as Del Ray, the saws and hammers of repair and remodeling are being passed from one generation to the next, as evidenced in a general sprucing up. Baby carriages are familiar sights along the sidewalks, and new stores are everywhere. A walk in Del Ray gives an idea of what Old Town was in the 1930s and 1940s, although change here is faster. The houses vary widely in type and style, from bungalow to Colonial Revival and Tudor Revival, and simple brick cottages of the 1950s; but for the most part, it is an area of small houses, with a rhythm of homey front porches along its tree-lined streets. Shops and restaurants lining a festive Mount Vernon Avenue symbolize the revival of the entire

district to the tastes of young suburbanites, who in Del Ray are only a skip from the District.

Rosemont

Planning for an "addition" began in 1891, but the development of Rosemont really got going only a few years before World War I and continued for over forty years. Vacant lots were still to be found in the 1970s, and only now are they disappearing for good. Bounded by Route 1 on the north and upper King Street on the south, Rosemont is a neighborhood whose early glory is its bungalows. On Cedar and Maple Streets the style is repeated in many different ways, from the classics, with their two or three battered wooden columns supporting gables that face the street, as in 6 West Cedar Street, to larger versions in brick, notably those at 5, 7, 14, 19, and 103 Rosemont Avenue.

But bungalows are not the only pride of Rosemont. A particularly beguiling section is found on Elm Street and Johnston Place, which wind between high banks topped by cottages of various kinds. Along West Walnut Street and Northview Terrace are Colonial Revival houses. Notable are the columned residence at 211 West Walnut Street and the shingle cottage at 210. The house at 203 Walnut Street, a fine Queen Anne cottage of a much earlier date than Rosemont, was moved here from Maryland many years ago. In buying the house across the street, a new neighbor realized that he had stood on the porch in 1894 while the house was still in Maryland and watched Coxey's Army of unemployed march by on its way to protest in Washington.

Northridge

The area northwest of Del Ray and Rosemont consists of a number of residential developments from the 1920s and 1930s—Beverly Hills, Jefferson Park, and Mount Ida—that were in their infancy when annexed by Alexandria in 1930. Shady streets wind over hills, at times steeply, on an elevation much higher than the riverside part of the town. The architecture spans all the styles, from English cottages to Spanish haciendas, but is generally footed in the Colonial Revival as popularized in suburban houses in the 1920s and heavily influenced thereafter by the Williamsburg restoration. Streetscapes are rendered more interesting by the variety.

In a 1914 bungalow in Rosemont, cobblestones pried up from Alexandria's old streets give an Arts and Crafts fireplace a "colonial" flavor.

Architectural enthusiasts will find this an interesting part of Alexandria.

Gardens in Northridge neighborhoods are mature, and the display of dogwood, redbud, and purple magnolia in spring and bright leaves in the late fall is dazzling. Since there are few fences and the cover of great old trees is very thick, summer makes this part of town a glade. The Washington area being as it is, there has been a tremendous turnover in the occupation of some of the houses. Congressmen, senators, and other government officials have been familiar residents of Northridge. Rocker Jim Morrison of The Doors spent his youth in the Jefferson Park area of Northridge. Old

cottages and farmhouses appear here and there. Central to the campus of St. Agnes School is Lloyd House, a towered summer villa from the 1850s, used as the school's central building.

Seminary Hill (Sites A–C)

Long before the town of Alexandria embraced it, Seminary Hill's heights were popular summer retreats, and the hills sprouted villas from at least the 1840s. It includes a number of suburbs, including Clover and Seminary Ridge. Central to Seminary Hill is the **Virginia Theological Seminary (A)**, with its elaborate central building, from the 1850s, and broad lawns. Founded in 1823 and housed first in St. Paul's Church in Old Town, the seminary moved to this site in 1839 and in the same year founded the Episcopal High School for boys, which is on the site. Phillips Brooks, the eloquent divine and author of the Christmas carol "O Little Town of Bethlehem," lectured to the faculty here in the late 1850s and remembered walking through deep woods from the railroad depot all the way to the sunny heights around the seminary.

The Seminary Hill area of Alexandria is almost entirely covered with residential suburbs today, most dating from after World War II, with the greatest growth in the 1950s and 1960s. Heavily occupied during the Civil War, it contained hospitals and temporary residential sections, notably those for newly freed African Americans. **Fort Ward (B)**, reconstructed in part from Mathew Brady photographs, stands on its original site at 4301 West Braddock Road. A museum within the headquarters building vividly describes Alexandria during the Civil War and is rich in original materials.

Sites of the other forts that dotted the ridge are not marked, as most fall in the yards of private houses. One such fort site is at 318 North Quaker Lane, but in this case, the house, historic **Clarens (C)**, although altered, has more to tell. It was the retirement residence of James Murray Mason, the firebrand heir apparent in Congress to John C. Calhoun. Confederate emissary to England, he was captured at sea aboard the *Trent* and imprisoned for the balance of the war. Jefferson Davis visited him at this house on October 29, 1870.

Alexandria's architectural climax, the George Washington National Masonic Memorial, completed in 1932, not only symbolized the distinguished past but signaled a reviving Alexandria, the beginnings of today's prosperity. Sited on historic Shuter's Hill, the monument offers spell-binding views of Alexandria, with King Street running from its base to the Potomac, and Washington and Maryland in the distance (pages 134–135).

A Spectacular View (Site 51)

No visit to Alexandria is complete without a visit to the **George Washington National Masonic Memorial (51)**. The site, known historically as Shuter's Hill, is the loftiest around. From the drive at the top of the hill the view is panoramic indeed, taking in the Potomac River, Alexandria at your feet, and Washington clearly in the distance. Reagan National Airport, started during World War II, keeps the skyline lively with planes, which from Shuter's Hill look like toys.

Tours of the Masonic Memorial include fine historical murals, some grand interiors, and an array of George Washington relics. The delight of every child is a miniature Shriner parade with hundreds of marching figures. The memorial itself is Alexandria's architectural salute to monumental Washington across the river, envisioned in the 1920s when Washington was undergoing a transformation in marble and granite. It was designed by Frank J. Helmle and Harvey Wiley Corbett of New York and built between 1922 and 1932.

From the Masonic Memorial, take a long look down King Street to the river, where Alexandria's story began. ■

Index

Italic indicates illustrations; **boldface** refers to tour information

A family enjoys a golden sunset on the Potomac River, at Jones Point.

◀ FRONT COVER: *Alexandria from the Potomac River. The original section, called Old Town, is one of the remarkable survivors of eighteenth- and nineteenth-century Virginia.*

BACK COVER, *clockwise from the top: Christmas parade in Old Town: fine eighteenth-century clock made by an Alexandria craftsman; young explorer rambles along the Potomac; Alexandria's First Citizen brought glory to himself and his town.* ▶

Office of Historic Alexandria, P.O. Box 178, City Hall, Alexandria, Va. 22313

Library of Congress Cataloging-in-Publication Data

Seale, William

A Guide to Historic Alexandria/William Seale

Includes index.
ISBN   0-9705419-0-2

1. History, USA–Alexandria, Virginia
2. History, USA–Architecture
3. Architecture, Virginia
4. Virginia, cities
5. Virginia, historic guides
6. USA, colonial sites

III. Title

00-109097CIP

Printed in the United States of America
Published by *The City of Alexandria 250th Anniversary Commission*
Photographs not otherwise credited
© Erik Kvalsvik, Baltimore, Md.
Designed by Viviane Silverman, *QuickSilver Design,* Falls Church, Va.
Maps by Shane Kelley, *Kelley Graphics,* Kensington, Md.
Produced by *Time Life Inc.*
Premedia Services by *Time-Life Imaging* and *DigiLink, Inc.,* Alexandria, Va.
Covers and gatefold by *Coral Graphics,* Hicksville, N.Y.
Text stock by *Warren Corporation*
Printed and bound by *R.R. Donnelley & Sons Company,* Roanoke, Va.

THE CITY OF ALEXANDRIA

<table>
<tr><td>2000–2003</td><td>1997–2000</td></tr>
<tr><td>Kerry J. Donley, Mayor</td><td>Kerry J. Donley, Mayor</td></tr>
<tr><td>William C. Cleveland, Vice Mayor</td><td>William D. Euille, Vice Mayor</td></tr>
<tr><td>Claire M. Eberwein, Councilwoman</td><td>William C. Cleveland, Councilman</td></tr>
<tr><td>William D. Euille, Councilman</td><td>Redella S. Pepper, Councilwoman</td></tr>
<tr><td>Redella S. Pepper, Councilwoman</td><td>Lonnie C. Rich, Council Member</td></tr>
<tr><td>David G. Speck, Councilman</td><td>David G. Speck, Councilman</td></tr>
<tr><td>Joyce Woodson, Councilwoman</td><td>Lois L. Walker, Council Member</td></tr>
<tr><td>Philip Sunderland, City Manager</td><td>Vola Lawson, City Manager</td></tr>
</table>

THE CITY OF ALEXANDRIA
250TH ANNIVERSARY COMMISSION

Bernard Brenman; Philip Brooks, *Chair*; Henry Brooks;
Susan Butler; Patrick Butler; Kim Ching; Kathleen Cummings;
Ferdinand Day; James Dorsch; Anne Edwards; Frank Fannon, IV;
Kenneth Foran; Lea Fowlie; Carlton Funn; Gail Gregory;
Philip Hays; William Hendrickson; Katherine Hoffman;
Ruth Lincoln Kaye; Robert Klausing; Anna Leider; William Monahan;
Robert Morrison; Kathleen Murphy; Michael Oliver; Laura Overstreet;
Kathleen Pepper; F. J. Pepper; George Pera; David Sachs;
William Francis Smith; Eve Stocker; Daniel Straub; Elsie Thomas;
Mark Underwood; Michael Wilkosz; Lowell Williams;
Richard Wyler; Robert Yakeley.

The City of Alexandria 250th Anniversary Commission thanks the
following for their support of this publication:

The Alexandria Gazette Packet
Alexandria Marketing Fund Committee
American Academy of Physicians Assistants
American Moving and Storage Association
American Society for Industrial Security
American Statistical Association
Mr. and Mrs. Philip C. Brooks
Burke and Herbert Bank and Trust Company
Mr. Patrick H. Butler III
Club Managers Association of America
Coca-Cola Enterprises and the Mid-Atlantic
  Coca-Cola Bottling Company

Commonwealth Atlantic Properties, Inc.
Fabrizio, McLaughlin and Associates, Inc.
The Fannon Companies
Inova Alexandria Hospital
Mr. Paul Jost
McEnearney Associates
The Honorable David G. Speck
Sugar House LLC
Vacation Spot Publishing
Wm. D. Euille and Associates, Inc.

CITY OF ALEXANDRIA,

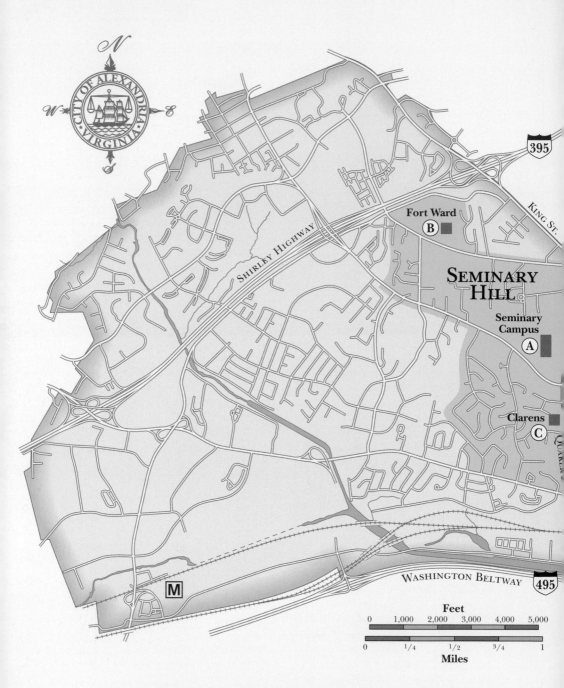

Map of the city of Alexandria, Virginia, showing the original
eighteenth-century riverside settlement, known as Old Town, and the subsequent
late nineteenth- and twentieth-century additions of suburban neighborhoods.

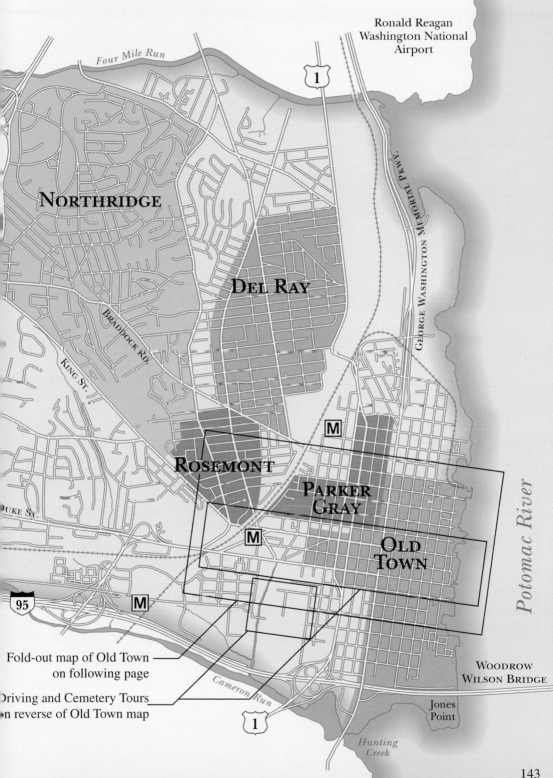

VIRGINIA

Ronald Reagan
Washington National
Airport

Four Mile Run

NORTHRIDGE

DEL RAY

BRADDOCK RD.

KING ST.

GEORGE WASHINGTON MEMORIAL PKWY.

M

ROSEMONT

**PARKER
GRAY**

Potomac River

**OLD
TOWN**

M

DUKE ST.

M

M

95

Fold-out map of Old Town
on following page

Driving and Cemetery Tours
on reverse of Old Town map

Cameron Run

1

**WOODROW
WILSON BRIDGE**

Jones
Point

*Hunting
Creek*

OLD TOWN ALEXANDRIA

■ Market Square and Environs

1. Fitzgerald's Warehouses
2. Ramsay house
3. Burke and Herbert Bank
4. Market Square
5. City Hall

■ King Street, West of Market Square

6. Site of the Marshall House hotel

■ Streets South of King Street, East to West

Prince Street

7. Confederate Memorial Statue
8. Bank of Potomac building
9. The Athenaeum

Duke Street

10. Slave Trade District
11. Caleb Hallowell School
12. Benjamin Dulaney house
13. Dr. Elisha Cullen Dick/ Kate Waller Barrett house
14. Dr. James Craik house
15. General Carl A. Spaatz house

Wolfe Street

16. Alexandria Academy

Wilkes Street

17. Railroad tunnel

■ Streets North of King Street, East to West

Cameron Street

18. Charles Bennett house
19. General Henry "Light Horse Harry" Lee house
20. Lord Fairfax house
21. George Washington's town house (reconstruction)
22. Duvall's Tavern
23. Cameron Mews

Queen Street

24. Queen Street Library (Kate Waller Barrett Branch)
25. Admiral William F. Halsey house

Princess Street

600–700 blocks

Oronoco Street

26. Robert E. Lee Boyhood Home

■ Streets North to South, Including Washington Street

Alfred Street

27. Black History Resource Center
28. Mechanics' Hall
29. Friendship Firehouse
30. Alfred Street Baptist Church

Columbus Street

31. Potomac Lodge No. 8, International Order of Odd Fellows
32. Christ Church

Washington Street

33. Old Cotton Factory
34. Lee-Fendall house
35. Lloyd house
36. Washington Street Methodist Church
37. Alexandria Lyceum

St. Asaph Street

38. Lafayette house

Pitt Street

39. St. Paul's Church

Royal Street

40. Gadsby's Tavern
41. St. Mary's Catholic Church

Fairfax Street

42. Jonah Thompson house
43. Lyle's (Kemp's) Tavern
44. Carlyle house
45. Stabler-Leadbeater Apothecary Shop
46. Green's Steam Furniture Manufactory
47. Presbyterian Meeting House

■ Waterfront

Union Street

48. Torpedo Factory

■ King Street, West End

49. Union Station
50. King Street Metro Station
51. George Washington National Masonic Memorial

CEMETERY MAP

Alexandria has many burying grounds. The cluster of cemeteries just south of Old Town represents the largest number of graveyards in one place and offers an interesting walk for visitors. Burials were not allowed in the town proper after about 1809, so these cemeteries were established, both by churches and by cooperative societies. Many fine old tombs, funerary art, and stones can be found here. Most parts are easily accessible by automobile, but to see some areas it is necessary to park and walk. Not shown on the map is the Union military cemetery, founded during the Civil War as a place to bury those who died in Alexandria's many army hospitals.

One of Alexandri
mysteries is the i
Stranger. Her gra
at St. Paul's cem
epitaph reprinted

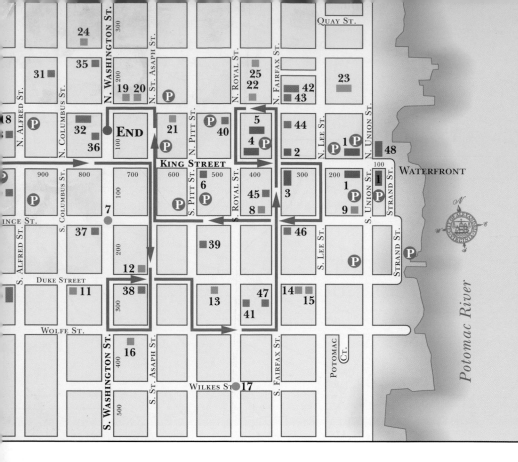

JEREMY J. HARVEY, ACVA

a's most enduring
lentity of the Female
ve (above) is found
tery and bears the
at right.

To the memory of a
FEMALE STRANGER
whose mortal sufferings terminated
on the 14th day of October 1816
Aged 23 years and 8 months.
This stone is placed here by her disconsolate
Husband in whose arms she sighed out her
latest breath and who under God
did his utmost even to soothe the cold
dead ear of death.
How loved how valued once avails thee not
To whom related or by whom begot
A heap of dust alone remains of thee
'Tis all thou art and all the proud shall be
To him gave all the Prophets witness that
through his name whosoever believeth in
him shall receive remission of sins.

Acts. 10th Chap. 43rd verse